Signs from

Above

Signs from Above

Your Angels' Messages about Your Life Purpose, Relationships, Health, and More

DOREEN VIRTUE
and
CHARLES VIRTUE

HAY HOUSE

Australia • Canada • Hong Kong • India
South Africa • United Kingdom • United States

Published and distributed in the United Kingdom by:
Hay House UK Ltd, 292B Kensal Rd, London W10 5BE. Tel.: (44) 20 8962
1230; Fax: (44) 20 8962 1239. www.hayhouse.co.uk

Published and distributed in the United States of America by:
Hay House, Inc., PO Box 5100, Carlsbad, CA 92018-5100. Tel.: (1) 760 431
7695 or (800) 654 5126; Fax: (1) 760 431 6948 or (800) 650 5115. www.
hayhouse.com

Published and distributed in Australia by:
Hay House Australia Ltd, 18/36 Ralph St, Alexandria NSW 2015. Tel.: (61) 2
9669 4299; Fax: (61) 2 9669 4144. www.hayhouse.com.au

Published and distributed in the Republic of South Africa by:
Hay House SA (Pty), Ltd, PO Box 990, Witkoppen 2068. Tel./Fax: (27) 11
467 8904. www.hayhouse.co.za

Published and distributed in India by:
Hay House Publishers India, Muskaan Complex, Plot No.3, B-2, Vasant
Kunj, New Delhi – 110 070. Tel.: (91) 11 4176 1620; Fax: (91) 11 4176 1630.
www.hayhouse.co.in

Distributed in Canada by:
Raincoast, 9050 Shaughnessy St, Vancouver, BC V6P 6E5. Tel.: (1) 604 323
7100; Fax: (1) 604 323 2600

A catalogue record for this book is available from the British Library.

ISBN 978-1-84850-026-6

Printed and bound in Great Britain by CPI Bookmarque, Croydon

We dedicate this book to Archangel Michael,
whose help, strength, and support allowed
us to have the courage to change our lives
in order to help others change theirs.

❖ ❖ ❖

CONTENTS

INTRODUCTION

Your angels are always with you and are always talking to you—especially in answer to your prayers. When life is stressful, you may not necessarily hear their soft angelic voices, which come in the form of intuitive feelings and thoughts. In those instances, these heavenly beings take their messages to a more concrete level and send you signs from above.

Signs are:

- Repetitive
- Out of the ordinary
- Personally meaningful
- Timed to coincide with your prayers or questions that you've posed to the Divine

Throughout life, we experience celebrations, challenges, hard times, joyous occasions, losses, and reunions. At times, even the most spiritually minded people can feel as if they're walking alone, without a helping hand. Yet since the angels are constantly around us, so is their guidance.

These celestial messengers are here to help us be peaceful and to guide us in helping *other* people be the same. Yet, the angels won't intervene without our permission or violate our free will. After all, we're here to learn and to evolve on a soul level, from both the good and the bad. Before we're born, we select a series of goals and lessons for our time on Earth. This is a form of sacred contract that determines what type of life we're going to live.

As a soul, you're destined to experience everything life has to offer. Whether you were born as an aristocrat or an average citizen, this lifetime is your opportunity to encounter what you need in order to develop on a soul level.

When angels help us through life, sometimes they do so in ways that may not be immediately recognizable to us. That is because they're here to guide and protect, not to lead and direct. They often deliver answers, hints, messages, and warnings through *signs*—signals, or anomalies in life, which let us know that they're with us. While this form of communication is as old as humankind, it's not widely known, understood, or recognized. The angels want to change this because signs are their most common and direct mode of getting in touch with us. They wish to help us all become aware of the fact that they're constantly sending us messages every day of our lives.

Today, you've already been shown several signs . . . and you're going to come across more before you go to sleep.

There are two steps to experiencing signs from above: (1) believe in them, and (2) notice them. While their magnitude and consistency vary from person to person and situation to situation, signs are abundant and are here to help us. Amazing life transformations occur when we learn to see and use the messages the angels give us in everyday life, in all situations, big or small.

As you read this book, you'll probably realize just how often the angels have sent *you* signs. Look back on the last major challenge you faced and recall any repetitive signs that you received in response to your prayers for assistance. How were you guided through? Were there any aspects of that particular situation or occurrence that just seemed to fall into place? If you answered yes, then you probably followed the signs you were shown.

Not all signs are small, and not all are monumental. Each one is there for a specific purpose, be it to comfort you, help you finalize a decision, or confirm something you already knew but weren't sure about. Following your signs not only guides you through situations, but also helps you make decisions that support your life path and goals. Paying attention to one sign leads to more, ultimately improving every aspect of your life and giving you the fulfilling and uplifting feeling that you're living with a purpose—*your* purpose.

Listening to your signs demonstrates to the angelic realm that you're open, receptive, and willing to be shown more . . . it encourages them to give you additional ones! If you ever feel as if the signs are eluding you, just ask your angels to show you something different or make their offerings more obvious or applicable to you.

Our job is not to *search* for signs; it's to *notice* them. The difference is subtle. Frantically seeking them out leads to tension, which makes angelic communication more difficult. By being relaxed about it, we keep our bodies and souls aligned with the angelic energy that surrounds, flows through, and protects all of us.

So just as you're letting the information in these pages be revealed to you, sit back and enjoy the show as you learn to ask for, see, and recognize signs from the angels.

While the variety of signs you might encounter is almost limitless, several forms they take have proven consistent and powerful. This book will guide you through examples of the more common ways in which Heaven delivers

messages, such as angel-shaped clouds, coins, feathers, rainbows, and meaningful songs. You'll also read true stories of how people were guided, protected, and healed with the help of the angels' signs.

Chapter One

CLOUDS OF HAPPINESS

Clouds are heavenly bodies of moisture, hovering above us like protective angels as they float around our world. Angels love to use these natural wonders to show us signs because they can be shaped in any fashion and are spectacular to look at. In this chapter, we'll explore how clouds are often used to send signs, messages, and feelings of comfort and well-being.

Our first example comes from Kathie Robertson, who received a sign from her "best friend" to let her know that they were never apart:

> Willie and I were best friends during the ten years we spent together. He was

a very large Border collie, with long black-and-white fur. Although Willie's size sometimes intimidated people, he was as gentle as a lamb. The kids always called him our "gentle giant." He had a beautiful, tender soul; and I loved him dearly. He was totally devoted to me and would sit on my lap for hours.

At the age of four, Willie developed epilepsy, and as the years progressed, so did the disease. In March of 2005 we finally had to say our good-byes. After Willie was gone, I expected him to visit me in my dreams, but months went by and he didn't appear.

Then I began going through a separation from my husband, and life became even more difficult. I asked the angels to give me a message in my dreams that would be uplifting and bring me joy. (In my mind, I was actually hoping they would tell me that I was soon to find a pot of gold at the end of the rainbow.) Instead,

I received my message after having lunch with several of my friends.

We were having a wonderful time, and when the meal ended, we all walked outside. As soon as we did so, I noticed a huge, milky-white cloud hovering impossibly close to the ground, approximately where the top of a telephone pole would be. This cloud was completely opaque except for a large midnight-black "crack" on the bottom. I called my friends over to look at this unusual sight, and as we stared at the cloud, it turned into my beautiful Willie! He was looking very regal, just as he had when he was young and healthy. I began shouting, "Willie, you've finally come to visit me!"

What a joyous and uplifting visit I had with my friend! It was the greatest message that the angels could have given me. In true angelic fashion, they let me know that my beloved Willie was with them in Heaven and was healthy and

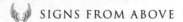

happy. And now *I* feel happy and at peace knowing that he's in their heavenly realm.

◆ ◆ ◆

Angels and departed loved ones frequently send signs, including birds, butterflies, and flowers; a unique scent that we associate with the individual who passed on (a favorite perfume, for instance, or cigarette smoke, if the person was a smoker); and even flickering television signals or household lights. However, clouds are one of the most common ways that we receive "I love you" messages from Heaven.

How many cloud formations holding comforting messages from departed loved ones do you think you've seen in your life? If you've been open to their presence, then chances are . . . a lot. Don't worry just because you may have missed a few—keep your eyes to the heavens, because the angels will stop at nothing to give you the messages you ask for and need. Carole

Edwards's story is a great example of how they use images of themselves to get attention and bring comfort:

On a cool, still afternoon in 2007, I was sitting on my lawn relaxing and gazing at clouds. One of them formed the perfect shape of an angel, a sight that filled me with awe and confirmed that Heaven does watch over us. The angel had large, full-length wings and was wearing a free-flowing gown. A beautiful wide smile was visible, and the figure's eyes looked like they were aimed directly at me.

Then the cloud seemed to melt away to nothing, leaving behind an empty spot. I scanned the opposite side of the sky and discovered another cloud in the exact image of my father looking at me. My dad had died suddenly in 2001, so this sight brought tears to my eyes. It filled me with a feeling of overflowing love and warmth and confirmed that my

wonderful father is still around, watching over me and showing me he cares.

This sight vanished just as quickly as the other one had, but now I'm filled with a renewed belief in angels and spirits. These glimpses have given me love, joy, and hope.

* * *

As clichéd as it may sound, looking up at the clouds when you're in distress can help you release whatever you're concerned about. The angels want to support you through the tough parts of life . . . and they can prove it. Next time you're feeling emotional, negative, or just plain upset, visualize all your worries being handed over to the angels. When you look up at the clouds, you'll feel as if everything is literally being lifted away from you, as Carolyn Ota discovered:

Two summers ago I was fired from my job. This was the second time I'd been terminated in less than two years; and at 50 years old, I was devastated, hurt, and angry. I just couldn't seem to let it go, and I was making myself sick with worry. I'd just finished the book *Angel Therapy*, but I didn't feel like I'd absorbed anything I'd read.

My husband was driving us from our home in California to a family reunion in Arizona. I tried to relax but just kept rehashing all of the negative nonsense in my head. Finally, I realized that I should just place it in the hands of the angels. I then put my seat back and looked up at the clouds. I saw beautiful heavenly angel shapes among them for the entire six-hour drive. A calmness came over me, along with a feeling of forgiveness for those who had hurt me. I felt as if I'd passed a milestone and now could go on with my life.

As a result of being unemployed, I was able to go on a monthlong vacation

to the Greek Islands with my family. This was something we'd dreamed of doing, which could only have happened if I wasn't working. When I returned home, I received three offers of employment and decided to take a job working at my daughter's high school. This in itself has been a true blessing!

● ● ●

We've all heard the saying "Problems are just blessings in disguise." It couldn't be more true, but until you recognize the hidden blessing within a problem, you may feel worried or depressed. Since we're all on a life path, events can only occur when we reach a particular juncture. Nothing can be rushed, and all timing is Divine. So while the answers may not seem apparent now, just ask the angels for a sign that everything will be all right. They'll be sure to show it to you, as Joe Hoftiezer experienced:

My youth was a very difficult and lonely time in my life. When I was in my early 20s, I attended community college and lived at home with my parents. I happened to pick up a book about angels and how to work with them. In one segment, it said that you had to ask your guardian angels to intervene in your life in order for them to help you. I did exactly that.

At this point I was in a great deal of emotional pain and, unbeknownst to me at the time, in the midst of a deep depression. I didn't expect anything to happen, but shortly after requesting the angels' help, something did!

I was driving to school up this big hill. It was very early in the morning, with the colors of the dawn still in the sky, when right smack-dab in the center of my field of vision I noticed this cloud in the perfect shape of an angel with her wings arched across the sky.

I felt such surprise and delight that tears came to my eyes. It had actually worked! The angels had answered me! I was on cloud nine for the rest of the day. The drama and beauty of that moment always brings a smile to my face. Things didn't suddenly become peachy-wonderful after that, but I did feel less alone and more full of hope. I knew then that the angels were real and were with me, and although I still had some dark times ahead of me, I could remember that incident and smile as the light of that moment came back into my mind.

* * *

It's amazing how some of our most random thoughts are actually messages. In the following story, Kelly-Sue shows that the angels can give us signs that help turn a seemingly tragic situation into one of healing and bonding. Seeing a cloud image allowed her to realize the gifts that life had brought her. Knowing that your life and those of the people closest to you have meaning is one of the most important gifts *you* can receive.

I was sitting out in the backyard, thinking about my mother and son. Deep feelings of love and appreciation came over me, and my heart expanded. I'd never felt such overwhelming emotion before.

I glanced up and noticed two clouds: they looked like a large angel holding hands with a smaller one. I knew that they represented my mom and son. I was stunned by the impact of this sight.

Two weeks later, my mother was diagnosed with terminal cancer. I became her main caregiver, and our bond deepened. In times of total despair, I'd remember the angel clouds, which helped me be strong for my mother. She passed five months later.

I went through deep sadness (as anyone would), and at times I still go there. But writing this has helped me know that my mom is safe and in the light. Her motherly love carries on.

● ● ●

The angels ask nothing more of us than that we believe and listen to their messages. Since they're not here to control our lives, sometimes their most powerful act is to comfort us. The angels' signs let us know that we're not alone and that we're on the correct path in our lives. Things that feel like monumental problems shrink to mere speed bumps when we sense the power and love of Heaven and realize that the angels are on our side, as Hiroko Iwasa's story illustrates:

My view of life has changed a lot since seeing angels in the clouds. Three years ago, I quit my job and taught myself how to conduct aromatherapy. Some months after, I obtained the qualification to start working at a private institution as an aromatherapy instructor.

I enjoyed teaching—until my students began dropping out and I lost income to the point where I couldn't purchase materials for upcoming classes. So I began supplementing my income by working part-time at a call center. It was a very stressful job, and my health started to suffer. My stress and health issues had a poor effect on my remaining aromatherapy students.

Eighteen months later, I was returning home from teaching, feeling despondent about my future. Desperate for help, I pleaded to my guardian angel: "Angel, please help me! I've reached the limit of my patience!"

I looked up to the sky and there were three clouds shaped like angels! They appeared as if they were about to fly down to the earth. My health began improving after that day.

Three days later, I received an unexpected prize—a complimentary deck of *Archangel Oracle Cards*—as well as an offer of free help publicizing my aromatherapy classes. With this answered prayer, I was able to quit my call-center job and dedicate myself full-time to teaching aromatherapy. Now that I'm aware of the existence of angels, my life has changed for the better!

● ● ●

As in Hiroko's situation, many people have been getting the message to quit their mainstream occupations and work in more holistic, healing roles. If you are one of them, you've probably noticed that the desire to be self-employed in a spiritually based career grows stronger each day.

When the angels ask for such a major leap of faith from us, it's often because we're here for a greater purpose, and the time to act upon it is now. Request that the angels show you a sign that this guidance is true and that it will all work out. Don't try to rush the answer; just ask and then live your life. The angels won't forget to show it to you in a way that's recognizable to you.

The angels' clouds are physical signs that they're with us around the clock. When we need the angels most, such as during periods of mourning, these beacons in the sky provide the reassurance that leads to healing, as Marge Jones recounts:

> My close friend Pat had been in the hospital for 57 days when she made the decision herself to be taken off life support. She'd been told that her heart was damaged beyond repair and even with a heart transplant she wouldn't survive.
>
> The day that I received the dreaded news from her husband, Bill, I was totally beside myself with grief. While looking

out the dining-room window at the sky, I clearly saw a cloud in the shape of an angel. I knew immediately that it was Pat passing over and saying good-bye to me. I then became calm and felt that she was definitely in a better place.

At nearly the same time, Pat's sister, Jackie, who lives 60 miles away, looked out her window and saw a rainbow in the sky. This sight was strange since it hadn't rained. Jackie also knew instantly that it was Pat's way of telling her that she'd made it to Heaven.

❦ ❦ ❦

Sometimes if we receive messages immediately after a prayer or see signs too readily, we discount them because the ease of transmission doesn't seem "mystical" enough. In this case, angels will hold off until just the right moment to show us that they're real and are with us. Sometimes the signs don't occur until we've almost lost faith, but keep in mind that their messages are custom-tailored for each individual and situation. Remember that you don't need special gifts to speak to and hear the angels; you just need to have faith, as Janet Ferguson discovered:

> I'd tried to contact my angels for quite some time, without success. I devoted each night to "angel time," where I'd sit and talk to them, use oracle cards, write them letters, or meditate and listen for answers.
>
> If I did receive a response, I'd quickly doubt it, convinced that it was just my imagination or wishful thinking. However, each day I'd continue to ask my angels for guidance, protection, and signs, always pleading: "Angels, I know you're there, but *please* just give me one sign!"
>
> My life was in turmoil at the time. I had troubles in my relationship, dif-

ficulties with my children and parents, and money issues. I became increasingly depressed but still hounded my angels for help.

After around six weeks with no angel signs, I began to think that I was wasting my time. I thought that perhaps I was holding on to a notion of something that just wasn't real. Having just come out of the spiritual closet, I felt foolish for believing. I'd been ridiculed by my partner for some time and began to think that he was right: there were no angels!

Yet, there was still a little part of me deep inside that just *knew* angels were real. I'd attended Doreen's seminar in London in June 2007, and I thought that all those people there couldn't be wrong!

So one morning I got up very early and looked out of the window as I began to talk to the angels in earnest. I told them all of my problems, worries, and fears. I asked for more faith and explained just how much I needed them. I requested that Archangel Michael clear away any blocks that were stopping me from seeing or hearing their guidance.

I literally *demanded* a sign that they were real and watching over me. I told them, "I need to know you hear me or I'm giving up!" Just then as I gazed out of my window, I saw the most amazing thing ever: there in the clouds was the massive shape of a male angel with giant wings coming from his shoulders. He sat on a throne with something in his right hand. The cloud was enormous, and sunlight was pouring through it. I immediately fell to my knees and started to cry. Tears streaming down my face, I watched the shape until it finally disappeared. As I looked at it, I felt love like I've never felt before. I just *knew* that things would be okay from then on. I believe that the cloud was Archangel Michael with his sword in his hand.

Since then, I've noticed lots of little signs that the angels are with me, and each gives me strength and purpose to go on. My relationship has suddenly started to heal, and life is getting better. I feel safe, loved, and protected. I talk to my angels frequently now. They are friends who never go away and are with me 24 hours a day, seven days a week.

If anyone reading this is thinking of giving up, *please don't!* It took me a long time to connect with my angels, but it was worth the effort.

❖ ❖ ❖

It's always so comforting to get messages that let you know that you're not alone. The following story from Dawn Simpson shows that the more you need solace, the bigger the angel cloud that's sent to you:

One night I was driving home from Boston with a friend and feeling very uncomfortable about navigating unfamiliar territory at 11 P.M. Nervous, I asked the angels to guide me safely home.

That's when I noticed a huge cloud in the shape of an angel over my car. I pointed it out to my friend, and she couldn't believe it. When I told her that I'd asked for guidance, she was excited because it was her first experience with angels.

❖ ❖ ❖

If you ask for their help and then believe in the messages they send (such as angel clouds), the angels can hold your hand through every challenging period of your life, as Sue Mazza recalls:

Every time life gets stressful, it seems that my angels send me comforting signs. For instance, on a difficult day at my retail job, a customer will walk up to my cash register wearing a shirt that says "Angel" on it, or some similar reminder.

Another time, an elderly man approached me and said that he'd save me a spot in Heaven—not now, but in a long time. His words seemed odd to me until I looked up at the sky and saw a beautiful pink cloud in the shape of an angel. When I glimpsed it, I knew that I was on the right path.

In addition to angel-shaped clouds, Divine guidance is often accompanied by feelings or impulses urging you to look or travel in unusual directions. Next time this happens, take a chance! You never know what Heaven has in store for you, as Sandy Mayor experienced:

I was at a metaphysical workshop, and I found myself facing my greatest fears. I called out for God and my angels to help, hold, and guide me.

That afternoon I experienced a breakthrough in class. As we left the building and crossed a busy street, something prompted me to step to the left and look up. I stopped in my tracks in the middle of the road . . . in shock and amazement. I began pointing at the sky, my mouth open but unable to utter a word. Then a voice burst out that I hardly recognized as my own: "Look up in the sky—it's a heart!" There was a huge, perfectly formed heart that looked like fresh skywriting. It was my sign from God and the angels that all was well and I was very much loved.

This was one of my first experiences of angelic intervention, and I still get a warm glow of love when I think of it.

❖ ❖ ❖

The angels let you know that you are special and loved. When you connect with them, amazing things can happen and you understand that miracles are real, as this story from Joy Roach illustrates:

> One morning I went out early to the garden porch of my apartment in order to say my prayers to start my day. The sky was overcast, and there were dark clouds in every direction. I recited my prayers and ended by visualizing the white light of the Holy Spirit surrounding me while I said invocations to the archangels.
>
> I tried to visualize each archangel filling my aura with a corresponding ray of color. When I was finished, I opened my eyes and directly in front of me was an opening of brilliant blue sky and a stream of bright light. The dark clouds were still to my left and right, but above me it was completely clear and cloudless!
>
> Even now it's difficult to describe the pure joy I experienced in that instant.

I truly felt blessed, and the positive emotions of those few precious moments remained with me for a long time. I look forward to more such experiences— not for validation, as I don't need that anymore, but rather for the pure joy of having them.

❖ ❖ ❖

The angels bring comforting messages from our departed loved ones as well. Very often these messages come in the form of signs such as angel-shaped clouds, butterflies, birds, or personal symbols. If you have any unresolved feelings or need to know that someone you lost is happy, just ask Heaven to give you closure, as Nancy Woodside did:

> After my father passed away, we scattered his cremated remains in a remote area in the desert where we'd camped in younger years. It's a really

beautiful place with different-colored hills surrounding it.

One day my husband and I went to visit my father's resting place. I walked up a small canyon alone to meditate and talk with Dad. I cried many tears and asked for a sign that we'd put him in the right place. As I looked up to the sky, which was only narrowly visible because of the canyon walls, I saw two vapor trails that intersected, forming a beautiful cross.

Then as if by magic the crescent moon came into view, looking like a big smile in the sky. And *I* smiled, knowing that we had done the right thing.

❖ ❖ ❖

If subtle signs aren't enough for you, the angels are happy to show you larger and more significant ones. Maria Marino needed an unmistakable sign, so that's what was delivered to her:

I asked the angels to help my twin sons get accepted to a wonderful "Divine" right school. Believe me, in Manhattan everyone with twins needs a miracle to get them into a good kindergarten. Well, the angels kept guiding me to be patient—until I thought that it was never going to happen!

I did see a lot of feathers on the ground as validation that the angels were helping behind the scenes. But with no school prospects in sight for my sons, I was really beginning to doubt that they were ever going to get in anywhere.

Then one night I was very clearly guided to step outside . . . and there, spanning the entire sky above our house, was a gigantic can't-miss feather cloud. It lasted about ten minutes and then was gone.

This was a perfect and unmistakable sign designed by the artist angels. After all, I'd asked for a clear sign from them!

Well, I got it! And the next morning, I received a call from the admissions director at a wonderful school. My boys had indeed been miraculously accepted!

The fact that Maria's cloud was shaped like a feather helped her relax and have faith. Feathers are a frequent sign that Heaven sends us, since we associate them with angel wings.

As you'll read in the next chapter, those feathers that you find mysteriously really do have Divine origins.

❖❖❖ ❖❖❖

Chapter Two

FINDING FEATHERS

Could you think of a more fitting calling card for an angel to leave than a feather? The angels place these special offerings in some of the most unusual locations. We've seen them inside indoor light fixtures, in automobiles, and even once on an elevator! Feathers may be the ultimate angelic sign. From our personal experience, they've served as a comforting confirmation of what we already knew with respect to a question or situation.

Although feathers come in all different sizes and colors, they're amazing signs because they're directly connected with the thought, prayer, or question that you had in mind. Rarely will you find one left by the angels without knowing what it means. Either you'll come across it while thinking about something or you'll immediately sense the association upon finding it.

This collection of stories related to feathers as signs from above shows us beautiful examples of how the angels want us to feel assured in our thoughts and intuition. We'll start off with Xanthea Hayes, who discovered that her feather was a sign for her to let go and trust in the Universe:

I'd just purchased my first new car, which made me worry about being involved in an accident, since I wasn't in a financial position to pay for any damage. So I prayed every morning for the protection of my vehicle and everyone traveling in it.

One morning when I was particularly stressed while driving to work, I noticed something attached to the sleeve of my shirt . . . it was a perfect white feather! I felt a wave of love wash over me as I looked at it. I knew that it had been placed there to remind me that I would always be looked after and was never alone.

There was no way that feather could have attached itself to me in the normal course of my morning. I don't have a feather pillow, we don't keep birds, and there were no other feathers in our yard or in my car.

❖ ❖ ❖

If you ever feel alone or abandoned, ask the angels to give you comforting signs of their proximity. Chances are, you'll be sent feathers, as Elizabeth LaFontaine explains:

> After living my whole life in the same city as my entire family, I'd recently moved to a new town. This was really difficult, as I was just starting high school. Suddenly, I was away from everything that was familiar to me. To top it off, my grandpa was in the hospital.

I took it day by day, but in November my grandpa passed away. I missed him so much because he'd always been in my life. I was also still adjusting to all the new things and people.

That's when I started to find feathers whenever I thought about my grandpa, especially on the days I felt a little sad and unsure of things. They were at my front door when I went out, and I'd find them on the road when I took a walk. Every time I came across a feather, it brought a smile to my face and warmth to my heart and remin-ded me that everything was all right.

I felt reassured, safe, and happy. I sensed that my grandpa was happy, too, and that everything was as it was meant to be. Thank you, angels and Grandpa!

Elizabeth discovered that she wasn't alone, and neither are you. You have loving and protective guardian angels with you at all times.

If you're having difficulty feeling their presence, ask them to send you a clear sign from above. Our next story, from Kathaline Schoonen, is a heartwarming example of how natural it is for children to associate angels with feathers:

A few months ago my nine-year-old son, Ezra, discovered his athletic talents at a school sports day in the park behind our house. At the end of the day, he found a beautiful large white feather, which meant a lot to him. He carefully placed it in his bedroom.

The next day my son had lunch at a friend's house. The friend's mother asked the two boys if they would like to pick an angel card from an oracle deck. Ezra concentrated and drew one that said: "If you find a white feather, your angels are very close to you."

He felt happy to have this validation, and when he returned home, he placed his white feather above his bed. Then our very old, sweet dog Pelle died. At the funeral, Ezra and I buried the precious white feather along with our beloved dog.

Ezra left the feather with his cherished pet and friend as a symbol of how the angels are always close. Most of the challenge in working with our angels and being open to their signs lies in the process of getting back to the uninhibited faith and wonder that children are naturally equipped with. We can learn a lot from our kids, as well as from trusting the angels and ourselves. However, when in doubt, we should watch for the signs, as Carmen Carignan discovered:

Whenever I feel confused, anxious, or overwhelmed, the angels always send me reassuring signs to let me know that I'm on the right path. Two years ago was no exception.

I'm a labor-and-delivery–room nurse in a small community hospital. Our women's health unit is unique in that we believe in noninterventional approaches to birth. As a result of this philosophy, we've become a leader in water birth, which is a very gentle method of bringing newborns into the world.

However, because the general medical community bases its practices on evidence, water birth has been deemed "experimental and potentially harmful" due to the lack of research about it. So, a small group of us decided to conduct our own research to support the fact that it's safe, which would be published in medical journals and presented in talks around the country.

As we were deciding how to go about this, we realized that we were taking on a huge project! Already two members of our team had quit, and we wondered if the study was more than we'd bargained for. We were sitting around a large conference table, with a pile of books about research. As we pondered whether to move forward, I noticed a very small white fluffy feather slowly descend from the ceiling and land right in the middle of the books! (Another member of our team also witnessed this.) A chill immediately went through my body. I knew in that moment that we needed to continue. The angels would gently guide us every step of the way.

It has been about two years. Statistics have been gathered, and the first phase of our project is complete. We've been asked to speak about it to the medical community on two occasions. Next, our research will be published in professional journals.

Thank God the angels gave us courage to keep going that day with that small feather! I'm still in awe, and very grateful for their gentle guidance.

Isn't it reassuring to know that the angels are available to you and every other person,

bringing peace and joy throughout the planet?
Karen Forrest shares a powerful story illustrating
just how responsive the angels are when asked to
show signs of their presence:

> My husband, Wayne, and I were
> traveling on an 11-day dream vacation
> to London and Paris. Halfway through,
> I realized that I wasn't engaging in my
> normal spiritual practices of meditating
> and using angel cards. I needed to know
> that my angels were still there, even
> while I was traveling overseas, so as I was
> touring the National Gallery in London,
> I invoked them by saying, "My guardian
> angels, I know that you're always around
> me, but I really need to feel your presence.
> Could you please give me a sign that
> you're with me by my side?"
>
> I continued walking through the
> gallery and immediately encountered
> two massive, exquisite paintings of
> Archangel Michael! Since he's the

archangel I most frequently call upon, this was very significant. I felt warm love spread through me. A couple of minutes later while still in the museum, a small white feather landed by my feet, and I distinctly felt the presence of my guardian angels!

The next day as we were touring the town of Bath, a large white feather fell in front of me. There were no others anywhere and no birds flying above me at the time. At least three more times that day, I found white feathers at my feet (including inside yet another museum).

At this point even my husband was noticing this phenomenon. Wayne commented, "What's with all these white feathers landing by your feet?"

I laughed as I explained to my husband that I'd asked for a sign that my angels were around me. Wayne simply smiled indulgently, knowing how I cherished my angelic connection.

Every time I picked up yet another white feather, I felt calm and loved.

These signs helped me feel more connected to Heaven. I also learned that no matter where I am in the world, my angels are always by my side!

● ● ●

Usually you have to ask the angels for a sign, since they respect your freewill choices. Yet the form of asking can be as subtle as wishing for some help and comfort. However you choose to request their assistance, the angels always come through in miraculous ways, as Aileen Kushner relates in this next story:

My mother, who has missed my father deeply since he passed, had gone in for minor surgery. She was nervous about the procedure, as she's not often ill.

Keep in mind that she was in a medical facility with top-notch cleaning procedures in place—everything was sterile and bright. As I approached her hospital room, I found a perfect white feather in the doorway. What are the chances of finding a feather several inches long in a hospital? I knew that my father was there watching over her.

My mom's first comments to me were about being uncomfortable with the situation and wishing she still had my dad around for support. I handed her the feather, explained where I'd found it, and reminded her that she wasn't alone and my dad would be with her through it all. And he was.

The angels and Aileen's father delivered the feather in a way that left no question about its meaning. Our angels and departed loved ones are more than happy to confirm their presence, and the timing is usually quite Divine. Although their energy is always present, we can feel even closer to our loved ones by asking them for a sign, as Sherry Krause did:

> I was feeling very depressed one day and asked for a sign from my first love. He had committed suicide the year before, and I was sad that he'd gone that way. I specifically asked him to send me a feather to validate that he'd heard me.
>
> Earlier that day, a landscaping company had left a big hole in our lawn. I grabbed a shovel to fill it in. As I went to dig, I immediately found a beautiful feather. I was so happy! But I still had doubts, so I asked for another. I filled in the hole and turned around to put the shovel away—and there was a second feather at my feet. And yet I *still* had doubts, since we have a lot of birds in our yard.
>
> So I apologized and asked again for one more feather. I walked into my kitchen, and what was sitting on the

counter? A feather! I burst into tears of joy. There was no way it could have "fallen" into the house! I finally let down my guard and accepted my sign. I also knew then that the other feathers were from Heaven as well.

Sometimes one feather isn't enough to make the loving impact the angels desire. When you need a *lot* of reassurance, don't be surprised if you're showered with them, as happened to Gina Cannella:

The worst winter day of my life was smack in the middle of my divorce. Seattle at that time of year is dark and dank, which made me feel even more depressed. After crying and screaming into my pillow all night, with very little rest, I walked out to my car to head to work. What did I find covering my old, beat-up Honda but hundreds of fluffy little white feathers!

Having studied some about the nature of the angelic realm, I felt tears well up (along with hope and joy). The feathers covered and encircled my car but weren't on the ground or anywhere else!

I cried, knowing that all was going to be okay and that I was loved and looked after. I picked some of the feathers off my car and put them in a plastic bag, which I placed on my front porch. When I got home from work that evening, the bag of feathers was gone. I lived in a secluded place at the time—no one would have come by, and if anyone had, the person wouldn't have seen the feathers where I left them.

The angels will bring you feathers and other signs in a way tailor-made to your own level of faith. They'll make sure that you understand the significance of their offering and believe that it's a real message from above. And sometimes, as in

Shelly's story, it's the way in which the feather appears that's significant:

> I'd felt exhausted and depressed for several weeks. I just wasn't able to cope with what life was throwing at me. I wondered if anyone actually cared about me, including my guardian angels, whom I appealed to for assistance. I really needed to know that they were looking after me.
>
> I settled down to watch television with my partner. Suddenly, I had an urge to look up. I saw a little white feather float down toward me from the ceiling! I put my hand out, and it gently landed in my palm.
>
> "Look—look!" I said to my partner. "It's a sign, the one I've been waiting so long for." There was no explanation for this feather's appearance. My partner doesn't believe in angels, but I think that this even shocked *him*.

From now on, I will never have another doubt. My angels are with me and care for me wherever I go!

When you feel the urge to make a big change in your life, you might worry whether it's the right thing to do. In such cases, it's a good idea to ask the angels for a sign from above to validate that you're being Divinely guided to follow your inclination, as Niki Leach discovered:

I was driving to work one morning, having doubts about moving forward with my plans to reduce my work hours so that I could focus on self-employment in my desired career area. A moment later, I turned onto the highway. Suddenly, I was surrounded by a cloud of white feathers swirling all around my car. I wondered whether the vehicle ahead had hit a bird, but there was nothing on the road to indicate this. When I looked behind me

in the rearview mirror, the feathers were gone!

When I arrived at work, I found the purest white feather attached to my car. I've taken this to be a sign that I should move forward with my business and have accordingly reduced my hours.

●●●

Whenever you see a feather, ask the angels for its meaning. The first thought or feeling that arises is your answer. And if you still need validation, keep asking the angels for it, as they're an inexhaustible source both of signs and of faith. Feathers and other signs help you know that you're not alone and never have been—or will be—as the following story from Mary Creech illustrates:

Nothing had prepared me, not even my job as a hospice social worker, for the painful experience of watching my own 58-year-old brother die of cancer. Although we'd always butted heads through the years, he and I were still close. Growing up with abuse, he'd been my protector. I never realized how hard it would be to lose that physical sense of protection.

After his death, I felt the need to go to the beach to rest and grieve. On the drive there, I met a Native American healer who told me, "Don't forget—if you find a feather, it means that the other side is making contact to say hello and let you know you're not alone." As I walked the beach on that first day, grieving and crying, I found a white feather floating in the water. I felt my brother's presence and experienced some peace.

I'd walked the Florida beaches for 30 years and had never before found a feather floating in the water. In the next three days, I discovered five! I knew that these were definite signs that my brother was still with me, protecting me and saying, "Hey, sissy."

Ever since then, I find feathers on my doorstep, sticking up in my yard right by my car, and even on vacation when someplace reminds me of him. Thus, I know that true brotherly love never dies, and when we need them, our loved ones give us blatant signs to let us know they're still with us.

Some of the best counseling you can receive arrives in the form of signs. After all, when it comes down to it, don't most of us just want to know that everything will be okay? Denise Dorfman shows us that confirmation that we're on the right path is just a prayer away:

I was going through a rough time in my life. I was finishing up graduate school and looking for a new job. I didn't want just *any* job; I wanted one that best utilized my talents and abilities. I was communicating a lot with Heaven using angel oracle cards.

One day while walking outside my apartment building, I found a feather in my path. I took it as a positive sign from the angels, and I said to myself, "Wouldn't it be nice if I found multiple feathers? Then I'd *really* know that the angels are with me!"

Sure enough, the next time I came around the west side of the building, I found 2 feathers, then 4, then 8 . . . and finally 16! This happened every time I walked in that area! I took this as a very positive sign of God's unfailing abundance. I was also told through the angels' cards that I'd get a new job in June of 2007. Of course, that's exactly what happened. Everything turned out all right, and I still receive signs to this day that the angels are always with me.

The signs from above give us encouragement that helps us keep moving forward during difficult times. As we've seen so far, this includes soothing grieving hearts that wonder how to survive their loss. The angels bring us comforting signs and reassurance that our love remains alive. And since we develop very close relationships with our pets, it's not surprising that the angels are compassionate caregivers for anyone whose heart aches for a beloved animal in Heaven, as Mary Schexnaydre discovered:

> My elderly cocker spaniel developed trouble walking. The veterinarian said that this condition was probably a spinal-cord compression caused by a tumor, which would lead to eventual paralysis. This did come to pass, and on my dog's last night at home, I stayed up and kept her company through the night. She seemed very aware of her condition. I told her how much I loved her and gave her a steak bone, which she enjoyed for a

long time. When morning came and the vet's office opened, I wrapped her up and brought her in. I signed the permission paper for euthanasia and held her as the vet eased her into a peaceful passing.

That night I went to work at the hospital where I'm a nurse. When I walked out to the parking lot the next morning, I was sad and weary. I reached my car and was startled to find dove feathers stuck to the driver's-side and passenger windows. I examined the cars parked on either side of mine, and there was not a single feather to be found. I immediately understood the message: my pet was just fine.

The angels' chief purpose is to bring peace to Earth, one human heart at a time. They help us with the big and the small problems in life, as long as that is the result. The angels know that when little stressors add up, we lose our sense of inner peace, so they're happy to point the way by sending us signs, as Karen Barnett's story illustrates:

> I'd finished shopping, with just enough time to go pick up my daughter, Alisha, from kindergarten. I was ready to drive off when I realized that my car wouldn't move because my hand brake was locked on! The roadside-assistance operator said that a repair truck would arrive at my car in 40 minutes. I felt panicked, as I had to pick Alisha up in 30 minutes and her school was a 10-minute drive away!
>
> I immediately asked for the angels' aid, saying repeatedly, "Please help me get to Alisha on time, angels, please." I stood at the side of the parking-lot entrance so that I could easily be seen, and that's where I saw a white feather float past and land near me. I thanked the angels for this comforting sign.
>
> I then received a text message from the roadside-assistance company,

explaining that they'd subcontracted my call to a local firm who'd arrive very soon. This helped ease my nerves, but I still asked the angels for another sign that I'd get to Alisha on time. I looked up to see a big truck pass by with a large white feather painted on its side! Five minutes later, the local firm showed up, and the guy released my hand brake straightaway. I thanked him and my angels for their assistance.

I got to Alisha's school with five minutes to spare! To this day, I've never found out the name of the company that had the large white feather as its logo, especially since there had been no other writing on that truck!

● ● ●

The angels send us physical signs in the form of feathers, along with other objects—such as coins—or living beings, like butterflies, birds,

and flowers. In addition to these tangible signs, the angels are great at getting our attention with music, as we'll explore next.

✿✿✿ ✿✿✿

Chapter Three

MUSICAL SIGNS

Scientists recently discovered that the earth emits a harmonic tone into the Universe. While undetectable to the human ear, this tone is our harmonic signature, and it comes from all motion and activity on the planet. Waves, seismic movement, and lightning and other types of severe weather all perform in an orchestra that provides the soundtrack to our existence.

So it's not surprising that humans love to make and listen to organized patterns of tones and harmonics. Music is one of the easiest things for our minds to grasp, as we have a natural knack for rhythm (some better than others, of course).

The angels often send their messages through the sound and power of music. It seems that almost everywhere we go, silence is replaced with music in one form or another—most of the time we don't even notice because it's so commonplace. Music can trigger memories or images of past events, people, or places. Pay attention, as recurring songs (or a series of songs sharing a theme) are almost always a sign from above.

Sometimes music can even be used to confirm the existence of the angels around us all the time, as Natalie Atkinson shares:

> A guy at my school named David asked me if I believed in angels. I told him that I didn't think so, and then he said cryptically that I'd soon come to know them. I was puzzled, slightly bemused, and a bit curious all at the same time.
>
> On the way home that day, I recalled how I'd been mistaken about some things in the past even though I'd been sure that I was right. So I pondered whether maybe my disbelief in angels was in the same category.

The next morning while I was driving to school, my car radio played a song about angels. I said silently, *Okay, angels, if you're real, I need a proper sign today— nothing wishy-washy, but a sure kind of sign that you're around.*

Although I love music, I get bored very quickly with songs. So halfway through the one I was listening to, I changed radio stations. To my surprise, another angel song was playing. The title was: "Angels Brought Me Here." This struck me as odd, so I changed stations again and heard two *more* angel songs in a row. This was beyond coincidence! Halfway through the second one, I switched to yet a different channel. You guessed it: another angel song!

I pulled over to the side of the road in shock and amazement. In that moment, I accepted angels into my life. They'd always been with me, but I was finally ready to acknowledge them.

David acted as an angel to Natalie by increasing her awareness of her celestial helpers and their musical signs. Your angels have undoubtedly spoken to you through music, too. If you feel or think that a song holds significant meaning, then it does. It's best to always trust your first impression when music triggers a memory or insight, as Jennifer Bonk and her husband discovered:

When my family and I were coming home from a recent vacation, we hit some terrible weather. My husband, James, was driving; and my daughters, Gabriella Grace and Angelina Faith, were trying to sleep in the back. The rain pounded the car, and I called upon the angels and fairies immediately.

As soon as I finished my prayers, the rain slowed and then eventually stopped. But the even bigger sign occurred a few moments later. During the downpour, we'd missed the gas station. On the

Pennsylvania Turnpike there can be 50 miles between service stations. Our car dash started beeping, and it stated that the tank would be empty after 36 miles.

My husband became worried, but I immediately started praying, since we'd just been helped with the rain. I asked for the angels to surround the car and safely get us to a gas station. Immediately afterward, a song by the band Warrant came on the radio, and the title caught my attention: "Heaven Isn't Too Far Away."

I told my husband that everything would be fine and that we'd make it to the gas station in time. He laughed when I explained that I knew this because of the music. He thought that I was nuts. But then the song that followed changed his mind. It was called "Knockin' on Heaven's Door," by Guns N' Roses.

Who would have thought that two songs about Heaven would come on back-to-back on a hard-rock station? My angels knew how to calm me, and we did make it to the service station with six miles' worth of gas left in the tank. Both my husband and I thanked the angels profusely.

Although Natalie believed in the angels, she required confirmation to accept the reality of their presence. While this occurrence is quite profound, remember that this isn't a privileged or once-in-a-lifetime type of event. The angels will show and confirm their presence to everyone who asks. And your request doesn't need to be formal. A simple plea for help is all it takes, even if you're just *thinking* about your desire for assistance.

If the angels see that you're in need of their guidance because you have a huge decision to make, they often volunteer their services to make sure you stay on your life's path. A woman named Shelly shares a story that demonstrates how the angels are always watching, and their help comes with Divine timing:

Every time my fiancé mentioned his job, I'd get upset for some reason. Since I couldn't put my finger on the source of my turmoil, I asked God to bring whatever was wrong to the surface. Soon after, I got the urge to check the voice mail on my fiancé's cell phone, so I did . . . and heard a female's coy message.

When I confronted my fiancé, he said that she was a co-worker who was attracted to him and had gotten his number from work. He claimed that although he'd asked her not to call, she continued leaving him messages. I didn't believe him, so I ended our relationship and gave him back his engagement ring. We both cried.

The next day, I was really hurt and felt bad as I recalled our relationship and how we'd planned to start a family. As I talked to God about my feelings, a mental picture came into my head of the two of us on a single path and me turning around and going the other way. When I glanced behind me, I could see my would-be husband looking back, and in the distance ahead of him were our children and a beautiful home. I could actually feel the presence of our unborn children with me at that very moment. I heard one of them ask, "Mommy, where are you going?"

This vision softened my heart toward my fiancé. I then turned on the radio, which was playing a song called "Listen to Your Heart," with lyrics that said to do just that before saying good-bye. I continued asking God to show me the truth and to give me signs about what to do. Almost every day I'd hear that same song.

Through this guidance, my fiancé and I reunited, and I learned that he was being completely honest about his co-worker's phone messages. Today we're happily married. We also became parents to the most beautiful little angel of a boy. God has blessed my husband with a new place of employment, which has brought more money and happiness. I thank God and the angels for showing me what I would have been giving up had I left the path.

This song was so significant that when my son inquired as to what I wanted for my birthday, I asked him to get me the CD that it was on, which he did. Six months later, he died in a drowning accident. I realized shortly after he passed that I would think of him whenever I heard the song, so I quickly associated it with him telling me hello. It never fails that the song will come on when I either think of him or feel as if I haven't heard from him in a while. For example, I may have the radio on very low in the van, and just as I turn up the volume, the song is playing. I always smile and sense that my child is talking to me.

They even played the song at a yoga workshop that I recently attended! It made me feel as if my son was telling me he was with me.

● ● ●

Remember that although bodies may pass away, the energy that connects you to a loved one is everlasting and can always be felt when you're open to receiving it. Since music is nonphysical, it's a bridge from your daily earthly life to the etheric energy of Heaven. If you hear a song that reminds you of a departed loved one, then it's a sign from above, as Shelly Pitcher experienced:

The Thanksgiving following my mother's death, I could feel her presence as my family ate our holiday dinner. Later that evening after everyone was gone, I was putting the dishes back into the china cabinet when suddenly I heard music playing! I stopped what I was doing to listen. I knew that I'd heard the tune before, but I couldn't put my finger on it.

Then I realized that it was coming from the little musical teacup that I'd bought my mom for her birthday several years earlier. The song it was playing was "I Just Called to Say I Love You"! Crying, I picked up the teacup and said, "I love you, too, Mom."

No one in my family believed me when I told them about this experience. Then I showed them that the only way to make the cup play was to push in the button on the bottom, which I'd never even gotten near that day, let alone pressed!

Since then I've had many more signs, and I'm grateful every day to know that my mom will always be around me! I *do* know that you love me, Mom!

The sound of the music itself doesn't always play the starring role. Sometimes the signs come from the presence of the band or musician. This music is usually not very lyric oriented and almost always involves original pieces performed by their composers. The meaning of these signs is rarely different from those delivered through the radio, but it's important to know that messages through music come in many different fashions.

You may also hear disembodied celestial music, which is sometimes called "the music of the spheres." Usually people hear this upon awakening, when their minds and hearts are relaxed and open, as Karen Anderson shares in the following story:

> The morning of my birthday, I awoke to hear a heavenly sounding chorus singing "Happy Birthday" to me. At first I thought, *Oh, my sons are singing to me from downstairs,* but I quickly looked at the clock and realized that it was much too early for my boys to be awake. I lay there in bed, stunned and excited by what I was hearing. Then I

began questioning whether the voices were my angels and departed parents.

I asked silently, *If I'm truly receiving a happy-birthday greeting from Heaven, please send me a sign.*

I got up and decided to retrieve the morning paper so I could read it while the house was quiet. When I opened the front door, there on my porch was a single red rose wrapped in a red satin ribbon. I giggled with delight and said to myself, *This flower must be my sign!* I later questioned my husband, and he said that it wasn't from him or the boys. So there it was: my special sign that Heaven was celebrating my birthday with me!

Karen was hearing the sound of the Universe and the angels, which plays continuously and naturally. Her groggy altered state allowed her to tap into another dimension, which she consciously remembered because she was nearly awake.

In addition to offering a connection to Heaven, music delivers very direct messages and signs. For instance, the title or lyrics of a song that you hear repetitively offer a chance to receive specific guidance from your angels. A few years ago when I (Doreen) was praying for guidance on naming my forthcoming book about food and appetite, I kept hearing the k.d. lang song "Constant Craving." After hearing it the fourth time in a row, I took the hint and used that title for my book of the same name.

In the same manner, Irene Felner needed guidance about whether to take a trip to Tahiti. The angels offered their support and messages through the medium of music:

> Three years ago when I'd made the decision to go on a Tahitian cruise with Doreen Virtue and James Van Praagh, I felt exhilarated, but at the same time a little nervous about spending such a great deal of money. I asked that a message be sent to me confirming what I already

knew in my heart: that this cruise was the right thing to do.

The very next day as I alighted from my train on my way home from work, I heard the sound of drums. The first thing that came to my mind was Tahitian drums. As I went down into the underpass, I saw the drummer, who'd never before been in that location in my experience.

For the rest of the time prior to my departure, the drummer would be there at least every other day. Once I returned from my cruise (which, by the way, was the most amazing trip I've ever been on) and went back to work, the drummer was gone, except for one day when I was again in a bit of a quandary. I'd asked for confirmation, even saying that it would be good to see the drummer again. Lo and behold, the very next day, there he was . . . but after that, never again.

If that wasn't a sign, I don't know what else it could have been!

* * *

You might be surprised to know just how many angels are listening to your thoughts when you put requests out into the Universe. This includes deceased loved ones—who are more than willing to give you signs and confirmation that they're with you. Kathy Johnson's story is inspirational because she so naturally discovered that asking a question and listening for the sign is all you have to do to get your answer:

> Right after my mom died, I was driving home from a little shopping errand and wondering which song I could sing to Mom each morning in order to keep her close in my heart. She had enjoyed music, loved singing, and thought that my voice was beautiful. So I'd decided that the first thing I would do every day was sing something as soon as I got out of bed. But what? Which song?

Just then, the radio played "The Mother Song," and some of its lyrics, paraphrased, are: "You won't feel me, you won't hear me, but you will never be alone." It's the words of a mother comforting her child before her own death—or maybe afterward. It was perfect, and it spoke directly to many of the emotions I was having about Mom being gone. I'd never heard the song before.

About a year later I'd just read a book about the deceased trying to give us messages and often being around us. I thought, *Well, Mom, I haven't seen any sign of you for a long time, and I'd sure like to. How about it?*

The next morning "The Mother Song" came on the radio again. It was only the second time I'd ever heard it. And I haven't heard it since.

The angels played the song more than once so that Kathy realized it was from her mother.

Once the message was accepted, the angels didn't need to keep sending it, but if Kathy ever needs reassurance again about her mother's eternal love, she'll undoubtedly hear "The Mother Song" again.

The angels will always be there to make sure that everything is all right. While life may put you in situations that lead you to feel isolated or vulnerable, you have to remember that you're never alone. Ask for help and signs when you need them the most, as Alison Lintonhi did during overwhelming circumstances:

> My husband, Colin, died of cancer when I was seven months pregnant with my fourth child. Before his death, I told him how devastated I was that he couldn't be with me when our baby was born, but he assured me that he'd be there through the entire process.
>
> When I was one week overdue, I had a very strong feeling that I might go into labor during the night. So I took

a shower, got prepared, and then said, "Right, Colin, if I'm going to have this baby today, you'd better be there, because you promised."

As I came out of the bathroom, I could hear the sound of lullaby music, but I couldn't locate where it was coming from. I eventually discovered the source: a baby light called a Lullaby Light Show that had to be physically wound up in order to work—and it was playing on its own! It had been in a cupboard and hadn't been used for about four years.

At that moment I knew that this was a definite sign that Colin was with me and I wasn't alone. I gave birth to a beautiful baby girl the next morning. All through the labor, I could hear my husband's voice encouraging me and telling me that he'd help as much as he could. I know without a shadow of doubt that I *was* helped and protected by God,

the angels, and Colin that day . . . and
ever since.

❖ ❖ ❖

No matter how they send signs to you, the
angels choose the best method to convey their
message, love, and support. Music bypasses
defenses and opens the heart, so it's a favorite
choice of sign from above. Yet sometimes you
may need something tangible to hold on to in
order to know that you're watched over and
loved. In these instances, don't be surprised to
find a "penny from Heaven," as we'll explore in
the next chapter.

❖ ❖ ❖   ❖ ❖ ❖

Chapter Four

PENNIES FROM HEAVEN

The Universe works in mysterious ways, and the angels are no exception. Sometimes their imagination leads to incidents that you may not instantly recognize as "signs." Well, as complex as our world is, it's not without patterns, and this chapter will help familiarize you with one of them.

Coins, or currency in general, are often used by the angels to show us messages or give us guidance. All aspects of this type of sign have specific relevance to you and your path, including the time and place you find the coin, its denomination, the message written on it, and the material it's made of.

In this chapter, you'll read stories that show just how variable the meanings of coins and currency can be, as well as the situations in which you find them in your daily life. Our first story comes from Melissa Patterson, who wanted confirmation and wouldn't take no for an answer:

On a lonely Christmas Eve, I was reading an angel book while walking on my treadmill. I read about a person who repeatedly found dimes and how this was a sign from above. The book said that if you wanted a sign from your angels, you just had to ask. So I asked them to show me that they were with me.

When my treadmill walk was done, I put the book down on my magazine rack. Lo and behold, there on the rack was a dime staring me right in the face!

The tears poured down my face. I looked around and said silently, *You are here with me! You are here!*

When coins aren't enough to drive the message home, the angels can resort to other currency-related measures. Sometimes when life seems hopeless and we're faced with one "bad" situation after another, the last thing we feel capable of is hope. When circumstances like this arise, only a concrete and blatantly obvious sign will do, as Amy Broderick and her sister Laura discovered:

My sister Laura and I were on vacation in Florida for my birthday. I hadn't seen her in a while, and we were catching up and having some deep, heartfelt chats. Laura was feeling low, and as we sat poolside, I saw an opening to share how the Universe responds to our requests. I told her that I'd been playing an abundance game and looking for loose change. Everywhere I went, I'd been finding money, and it was really fun. I further mentioned that it didn't have to be coins; it could actually be paper money. She smiled and took in what I was saying; however, I could tell she didn't really believe me.

A little while later, we were getting hot and headed to the pool for a dip. As Laura stepped down into the water, I saw her reach toward her foot. She said that something was between her toes. Much to both of our amazement, she pulled out a folded-up $20 bill that had been lodged there. The look in her eyes was absolutely priceless . . . but the signs didn't stop there.

Later in the day we were walking around the resort, and Laura was talking to me about how depressed she was over how her life was going. I put my arm around her and told her how much I loved her. I also let her know how much *God* loved her and that she could move past any hurdle, if she could just really believe that.

At that moment we noticed a skywriting airplane above us. I was curious and said, "Oh, let's see what it's going to say." As we watched, the plane wrote: "God Loves You." Once again Laura looked at me and marveled at the synchronicity of the message.

I just smiled in appreciation of the extra love and support that God and the angels provide!

Whether you need a sign for yourself or for a loved one, the angels are always happy to oblige. Oftentimes the placement of a coin holds special significance, as you'll read about in the following story from Carole Renaud. The angels' sign allowed her and her husband to enjoy the vacation of their dreams:

While on a trip to Las Vegas, my husband and I decided to take a small-aircraft flight to see the Grand Canyon. While the thought of flying in a tiny plane over the vast expanse of the canyon was frightening, it was something that we really wanted to do.

The morning of our Grand Canyon tour, I asked the angels, including Archangel Michael, to fly with us to ensure that we were safe throughout the trip. When we boarded the airplane, there on our assigned seats were two brand-new pennies!

When I saw the coins, I knew that our guardian angels were on the plane with us. This realization helped us relax and enjoy the ride. The whole experience, both knowing that the angels were with us *and* the spectacular view of the canyon, was beyond words.

To this day, when I think of my trip to the Grand Canyon, I reflect on those two pennies and thank my angels for being along for the ride.

Although the angels would have been on the flight regardless, the comfort and reassurance that the coins brought through such undeniable confirmation was worth more than gold. The angels devise their signs perfectly for each person and situation. Elizabeth Gustafson's story depicts how even at the moments we feel the lowest, the most obscure find can be a message of joy in disguise:

One week before Christmas, I was laid off from my job. This came as a shock, since it was during the holidays.

I gathered my belongings and forlornly walked to my car. Then something on the ground caught my eye—it was a penny! I picked it up and decided that the coin must hold some significance. I discovered an hour later what the penny really meant.

I received an e-mail from a friend that gave me chills as I read it because of its synchronicity. The friend told me about a well-to-do man who had invited one of his employees and his wife to spend the weekend with him. They were going out to dinner, and the female guest watched as her husband's boss bent down to pick up a penny on the sidewalk outside the restaurant. She thought that this seemed strange, since the man was so wealthy, but she assumed he had a coin collection.

During dinner, the lady couldn't help but to bring up the coin that she'd seen her host pick up. He kind of chuckled and took it out of his pocket. As he looked at it, he asked her if she knew what the writing on the penny was. She thought for a few moments and admitted that she couldn't think of what it was. The man told her that it said: "In God we trust." He explained that every time he saw a penny on the ground, it told him that God is trying to get his attention and have a conversation with him.

When I read that story, I couldn't believe the wonderful and heartwarming synchronicity that it held for me on that dark day. God wanted me to know that while things may have seemed very cruel, soon I'd have a reason to smile again. As it turned out, I was about to find the most wonderful job of my life, working in the accounting department at Hay House (the company that is publishing this book).

Coins from Heaven don't necessarily have to be currency. In fact, the following story from Lisa White shows that "angel coins" can convey exactly the right message to someone in need of comfort:

I was on my way to work, feeling sad, discouraged, lonely, and overall very negative. I was feeling cut off from our

Creator's love (which I knew was my own doing).

As I pulled out of my driveway and headed to the mailbox, I asked God to send me a sign that I was loved. Feeling very emotional, I had tears in my eyes as I stopped at my mailbox. I took a deep breath, got out of my car, and retrieved the mail.

As I turned around, I just happened to look down. There, sitting right in front of my shoe, was a gold coin. I knew that it was special—not due to any monetary value, but due to great personal value. My heart raced with anticipation as I bent down to pick it up.

I could hardly believe my eyes when I read the words *Guardian Angel, watch over and protect us* on the front. The flip side had an image of an angel on her knees, with her hands folded together in prayer. I started to cry, immediately feeling loved and protected by our

Creator. This coin is near and dear to
my heart, and whenever I'm feeling
down, I hold it and feel love from God.

Lisa's experience would ultimately change
her life for the better because she no longer
doubted the presence of her loving guardians,
the angels.

One of the most fundamental lessons in
communicating with your angels and God is
that no problem is too small, and no request is
considered petty. Some people fear that if they
ask for Heaven's help with something "small,"
they're taking away from other more important
issues in the world. Yet no task is too trivial, and
no request is unimportant to God and the angels.

Jessica Nielsen's story illustrates that the only
thing that stops you from being helped is your
reluctance to ask:

I'd recently returned to talking
to God after a long period of being
indifferent. I was still overcoming my

religious upbringing, which had taught me to feel ashamed of myself and preached that God would only help me with the big—not the little—things in life. To overcome this early training, I talked with the Creator a lot, as I figured that this was the best way to develop a relationship with Him.

One day I went to my college's vending-machine area because I was really thirsty. I was five cents short of having enough change to buy a drink. I had money, but the machines didn't take dollar bills, so I begged aloud: "Come on, God, just one more nickel!"

I heard a *plink* sound and then looked down at my feet. There lay a shiny little dime! I looked around and didn't see where it had come from, and there was no way it could have fallen out of my wallet because I'd looked through it thoroughly. So I picked the coin up and—a little shakily—said, "Thank you."

I think God was trying to tell me that He's always there, even for the little things. Plus, I got to keep the change from the dime!

Life teaches us lessons that give us wisdom, and it seems that the older we get, the less afraid we are to acknowledge messages from above. In Anna Robilotto's story, her father and the angels worked as a team to make sure everyone would know that death couldn't keep him from loving his daughters:

Before my father passed away, he'd been able to spend time with his five children. My sister told him that she and her daughters were saving their dimes to take a trip to Italy. Dad's reply was: "Take care of your dimes and your dollars will take care of themselves."

As we were climbing into the car for my father's funeral procession, my sister's daughter reached into her coat pocket

. . . and pulled out a dime! She was so delighted when she told all of us: "Look! A dime! It must be from Grandpa!"

Before the day was through, almost all of us had found a dime in a pocket.

On another occasion when I was having a health challenge, I asked for a sign that everything would be all right. Then I stood up and something fell out of my lap. When I looked down, I was amazed to see that it was a dime!

I know that my father is watching over my family and me.

The next time you find a coin on the ground, know that it was purposely placed in your path. The angels realize that we love to receive gifts, and the gift of a coin helps us feel supported—financially, emotionally, spiritually, and physically. Coins are a reminder of the

Universe's infinite abundance of all that is good.

The next chapter discusses a time-honored sign that—like found coins—brings a smile to everyone's face.

Chapter Five

FOLLOWING RAINBOWS

Since the time of Noah's ark, rainbows have historically been symbolic of God's promise of love, care, support, and protection. And because the angelic realm is made up of love and light energy, it's not surprising that Heaven gives us visually stunning signs in the form of rainbows.

A rainbow can appear in the sky, reflected from a crystal, within a puddle, or in photos and paintings. When you ask the angels for a sign and you see a rainbow, it signals that your entire situation is being taken care of by them. This is a calling to completely let go so that they have the freedom to steer things the way they're meant to be.

If you need additional validation and confirmation, the angels are more than enthusiastic to provide extra signs, as Silvia T. experienced:

> I was at a crossroads in my life and didn't know which direction to go. So one day while I was driving, I asked my angels to show me a rainbow as a sign to help me decide what to do next.
>
> Mere seconds later, I saw a big billboard on the side of the road that said: RAINBOW ICE CREAM. I was excited but still wondered if it was a coincidence, so I asked my angels for another rainbow sign.
>
> While I was walking home that very same day, I saw a clear rainbow shimmering in a puddle of oil. Throughout the day I kept asking for more rainbows, as I really wanted to be sure before making a big life decision.

When I got home, my daughter Taylor spontaneously drew me a picture of a rainbow, so that day I received *three* such signs! I quietly thanked my angels for them, because they helped me let go and trust.

Fortunately, Silvia was open-minded enough to realize that a particular sign can come in many different varieties, as her three rainbows illustrate. In this next story, Stephanie Black shares how a rainbow became the calming miracle that she needed at exactly the right time:

When I was living at home with my parents, there was a lot of conflict in the household, sometimes to the point of violence.

I asked archangels Michael and Raphael to intervene on my behalf, because I wasn't sure how much more of my family's arguments I could take. That afternoon I was feeding my mum's horses in our westerly paddock when I looked up through the fog and saw a beautiful albino rainbow (an arc of white light sometimes seen under hazy conditions).

I was flabbergasted! I'd just read an article about albino rainbows. I hurried to point it out to my mum, but she didn't seem to hear me and the rainbow faded. Apparently, it was a message especially for me. Later when I went into the house, I retreated into the healing room for some peace and quiet away from the conflict. I hadn't been there for more than a minute when my parents (who'd barely spoken to each other for a week) walked into the room hand in hand and announced that they were going to work together to sort things out.

I thought that they were joking. Then I heard the angels whisper in my ear about my earlier prayer to Michael and Raphael and their sign in the form of the albino rainbow.

My family's problems haven't ended, although things were easier for almost a year after that. It was certainly a miracle that I'll never forget!

Albino rainbows, double rainbows, and moonbows (rainbows appearing at night under the moonlight) are all so unusual that they leave no doubt as to their significance. When three rainbows appeared simultaneously, it surely caught Tracy Jones's attention and brought her much-needed comfort:

During my pregnancy with my third child, every medical test yielded alarming results, so I was sent to a specialist, who told me that my baby girl would likely be born with Down syndrome. While we were at the clinic, the doctor strongly recommended a testing procedure. However, we were told that the test had the dire side effect of terminating 1 in 50 pregnancies. I refused to take it because I didn't want to harm my baby. I knew that I'd care for and love this child either way, so I just couldn't risk it.

However, I was anything but calm. My thinking was erratic, and my heart and thoughts raced. On the drive home from the doctor's office, my mother insisted that I slow down. I looked at my speedometer and I was going more than 90 miles per hour and hadn't even realized it. Then I began crying and wondered how I was going to care for this child with two other little ones and a full-time career.

Suddenly, I was filled with this incredible feeling of peace. I looked up in the sky: it was covered with three full rainbows, which spanned all visible areas. My mother and I were amazed. It didn't seem possible, as it hadn't even been raining. We had never in our lives seen the entire sky covered with rainbows, and certainly not on a perfectly clear day.

As we drove through those rainbows, we immediately felt the peace of knowing that God was in control and we needed to have faith. I still believe that angels were with us that day and that a higher being took control. I felt their presence for the remainder of my pregnancy.

Months later, I brought home my perfect baby from the hospital. She has absolutely no medical concerns. The doctors and my extended-family members were visibly relieved. My mother and I already knew, because God and the angels had given us such a clear sign with the rainbows!

What a heartwarming way for the angels to reassure Tracy! They knew that it was healthier for both Mom and baby if Tracy was calm and happy throughout her pregnancy. The resulting miracle is a prime example of how God and the angels communicate their love to us.

The timing of rainbows is one of the more remarkable aspects of their presence. I (Charles) have yet to meet someone who asked for a sign, saw a rainbow, and continued to doubt. It doesn't even have to be raining for one to appear. When the angels want to show you a rainbow, it will appear and you'll be guided to see it, as Lisa J. Wood's story illustrates:

I was struggling to leave a toxic relationship because even though I knew my partner was all wrong for me, I still loved him. So although I broke up with him, I was very conflicted.

One day I made the decision to delete his photos on my cell phone as a symbol of letting go of the relationship. A few minutes after I did so, I felt drawn to a nearby window around the corner. As I peered out, the most brilliantly bright and incredibly arched rainbow was right in front of me, although there had been no rain!

I felt that it was a sign validating that I'd done the right thing by letting the relationship go. I felt incredible relief and peace.

Rainbows are not only signs, but also gifts of encouragement and guidance from the other side. We sometimes receive these signs even when we know we're on the right path, and they serve to bless us with the same joy and beauty that rainbows are created with. Kathy Shogren's wonderful story portrays how our departed loved ones can send us beautiful reminders that they're with us and approve of our actions:

My beloved Airedale terrier Rose-bud passed away in my arms following a long illness. After her death, I'd talk to her in Heaven. Rosebud knew how much I missed her and how I needed to have a dog in my life, so I asked her to select my next one for me.

The next thing I knew, I was guided to look on an Airedale Website that featured rescued dogs in need of good homes. I wasn't really browsing it with the intent of immediately finding a new pet. Something just nudged me to look there.

But when I saw a picture of Jake and Molly, brother and sister rescue dogs, I knew on some level that these were the ones that Rosebud had chosen for me. Jake and Molly were mixed breeds, so they'd be difficult to place. They needed us and we needed them, as my husband, Randy, and I were heartbroken over Rosebud's passing.

So we made arrangements to adopt Jake and Molly. On the day that we went to get the dogs, Randy came into the room all teary-eyed. He said that he couldn't believe it, but there was a beautiful, expansive double rainbow outside! While *he* was amazed, I merely smiled and said matter-of-factly, "That's because Rosebud sent one rainbow for Jake and one for Molly."

I knew this was her sign that she was safe and happy in Heaven and we had her blessing to move on and give our love and a great home to the dogs she had selected for us. This year we'll celebrate six glorious years with our "furkids," who are wonderful, angelic creatures themselves.

How comforting the double rainbow was for Kathy! If your heart is heavy with grief, you can ask the angels to send you a sign from your loved one in Heaven. They will select exactly the right one to convey your friend or family member's eternal love. And sometimes, the sign may come in the form of a voice, as we'll examine in the next chapter.

Chapter Six

HEAVENLY VOICES

As the stories so far have illustrated, when you receive a sign, you can sense its meaning. You just know or feel its significance in relation to your questions and issues. Yet sometimes (such as in an urgent situation), the angels communicate in a plain-as-day fashion so that no misunderstandings or ambiguities are involved.

When there's an impending emergency or an excess of personal stress, the only way that the angels can ensure you'll hear them is through direct verbal communication. And if the angels talk, there's no doubt as to their message and meaning, and you should definitely listen.

"Hearing" can be defined in a few ways. Most obvious is actually audibly discerning a voice or a message, as if someone were physically speaking to you. Next is a sort of internal hearing, where you receive messages in your mind. They can feel as if they were spoken out loud, but they come from within.

We've all been taught that hearing voices is a sign of insanity, but as you'll read in this chapter, listening to the words of an angel is often the sanest thing that you can do. Our heavenly guardians are always talking to us, usually in whisper-soft tones that we feel rather than hear. However, in times of trouble, the angels speak up loud and clear . . . and their voices give us signs and guidance as to what actions to take.

When Linda Pullano experienced internal bleeding following her surgery, her angels were right there to verbally and physically help:

> After my hysterectomy, I spent the usual time in the recovery room and was then transported to my private room. I

don't know how long I had been there when suddenly I felt an intense explosion in my stomach. I was in excruciating agony, which is unusual for me since I have a very high pain threshold, so I knew that something was really wrong.

I immediately started reciting the Lord's Prayer with great reverence and pleading. Immediately, a bright light surrounded my entire being. I felt like I was in a bubble of protection, love, healing, and calmness. I was free of pain!

I was awestruck and filled with bliss and peace, and I knew that it was God. I also knew that I was loved and that I mattered. Then a voice said, "Those are the prayers you're feeling."

The voice repeated this statement five times before I answered. I knew that I was listening to an angel. I then said to this angelic presence: "I always knew that prayers worked, but I never knew that you could *feel* them." Then, almost in a grand finale, the voice repeated the exact same statement once more with absolute command and reverence. I felt so grateful, humbled, and loved at that moment that I will never, ever forget it.

The angel then relayed to me that I could heal myself. The funny thing is, at that time—in that state of God Light—I knew that the angel was right: I *could*. I was then directed to pull light into my head and down into my belly. I did as I was told.

As I pulled light into my head and then into my stomach, I witnessed incredible healing. I didn't know at that time that this was the case, but I knew that something Divine was occurring. I saw everything that went on. As the radiance came through my body, it looked like a huge light in a dark theater. The column of light came down, and you could see the massive tower but also the little filament particles within. This was pouring through my head into my stomach and then turning into billions of God-light particles.

I know this sounds weird, but the light particles had mouths (like in the video game Pac-Man), and they started chewing up something in my stomach. (I didn't know until later that it was blood they were consuming.) They all had intelligence, and each had a mission. The grand mass of the light tower was also intelligent.

This light tower poured through my head with intense speed and power. It was so loud that I had to cover my ears. It was incredible. While this was occurring, I still continued to pray.

Then the event was over, and I saw that the doctor was sitting at my bedside, looking frightened. He yelled, "We have a bleeder!" which meant that I was hemorrhaging internally.

While the nurse injected a tube into my arm, the doctor explained that I'd need an immediate blood transfusion. I told him that he didn't have to operate on me again. He informed me that after my blood level was restored through the transfusion, he'd perform a second operation to stop the internal bleeding.

I repeated that a second operation wasn't necessary because I'd experienced a miracle healing. I also said that as a professional singer, I couldn't afford to have my stomach cut.

The doctor replied that he had no choice. I told him that if he cut my stomach, I wouldn't be able to sing. Well, I could tell that he was thinking that without the operation, I might die, which would *definitely* stop my singing. But with my entire being, I knew that I was fine. I recognized that I had experienced the most extraordinary miracle.

The doctor then patted my arm and told me he'd see me at 7 A.M. in the operating room.

The next morning, he came to my bed and said, "Linda, the human body is a miracle machine in itself. Somehow your body stopped its own bleeding!"

I then said to him, "I know—I told you that last night."

The miracle left me on cloud nine. It was a Divine intervention for my own spiritual growth.

Linda's life was saved by the angels, and this was confirmed through their loud and clear messages to her. Sometimes Heaven gives us just enough information to allow us to figure out our next step for ourselves, as Atherton Drenth discovered. When she continually received signs in the form of scarabs, it took an angelic voice for her to understand their meaning and discover her true home:

Ten years ago I had a dream in which I woke up to find a very large sore on my right cheek. When I opened it up, a huge mother-of-pearl scarab slipped out of my face. It shocked me so much that I sat up with a gasp, wide-awake. The dream really shook me up, and I spent the next year and a half thinking about it every day and wondering what it meant.

I asked a lot of people what they thought its significance was, and they all said the same thing: "What does it mean to *you?*" It was very frustrating and not what I had hoped to hear!

One day my husband and I decided to drive into Toronto with the children to go see the Egyptian-artifact display at a museum. As we walked around looking at all the artifacts, we came to a display that showed a model pyramid. At the base were lots of scarabs, with a sign that said: "Scarabs were given to initiates to signify their awakening to the mystic journey." I was stunned.

Sometime later, I was shopping for a house. Although I worked very hard to get one, all the doors seemed to be closed.

One day I ran into a friend who asked, "Have you found your house yet?"

I just sighed and said, "I give up. I've had enough—no more looking or trying!"

That's when everything changed and the doors started opening for me! Five minutes later, I was driving up a street when I saw a FOR SALE sign and heard a little voice say: "That's the house." I slammed on my brakes, parked the car, and pulled out my cell phone to call my real-estate agent. Now, he's a very busy guy who's never in his office, so imagine my surprise when he picked up the phone! I said that I wanted to see the house, and he got me an appointment that night.

The minute my husband and I walked into the house later that evening, I knew this was it. Yet I worried about the cost. As I walked around upstairs, I called upon Archangel Michael, saying to him, "If I'm really supposed to go through with this, then I need tangible proof from you. I need something in my hands that I can hold on to—something that I can hold and keep so that I know without a doubt that this house and that vision are the truth and we are being guided through this."

I heard a voice say, "Look in the corner." I turned and right there on the floor was a jeweled scarab pin. That's when I knew. Two hours later our offer on the house was accepted! Every day it's an honor and a blessing to be here in this home.

The scarabs were markers along the trail that led to Atherton's dream home. Once she realized that they meant she was on the right path, she was more likely to notice the many ways in which they appeared to her. Every individual's signs and symbols are uniquely personal, but if you don't see or understand yours, be sure to ask your angels. And as Julie Annette Bennett discovered, it's important to listen to the signs as a way of staying safe:

At age 24, I was single, and life for me was working Monday through Friday and then going out on the town Friday and Saturday nights. Together with my friends, we'd drink and dance the weekend nights away. Our favorite dance spot was the Red Onion in Woodland Hills, California.

One Friday morning, I awoke at my usual 6 A.M. Groggy from too little sleep, I plugged in the coffeepot and got into the shower, thinking about the night to come. I could already feel the beat of the music as I pretended to dance with a not-so-eligible man from my office. Suddenly, a loud inner voice from deep within said: *Don't go tonight!*

Why not? I thought back just as quickly.

Just don't go tonight, the voice seemed to respond in my head.

As I got ready for work, I also selected an outfit to wear to the dance club in the evening. Once again, I heard the voice say, *Don't go tonight!* A little annoyed with this persistent message, I decided to bring the clothes with me anyway, just in case I decided to go out after work. All day long the voice repeated its warning, but I was young and headstrong, so I ignored it, determined to go out dancing.

At 5 P.M., I left my office to drive to the Red Onion dance club, despite the voice continuing to warn me as I headed toward Woodland Hills. Dressed to make heads turn in my seductive lacy blouse and short skirt, I wandered into the Red Onion. My girlfriend Pat was waiting for me at a table, and we ordered drinks. She and I left our table in the hands of Ken, a co-worker and friend, in order to use the restroom. We knew that there would be no more room for standing, much less sitting, very shortly.

As I sat on the toilet in privacy, I felt fear grip my whole being. Silently I prayed, *Please, dear God up in Heaven, whatever happens tonight, don't let me die.* Feeling a little better, I strolled with Pat back to the table where Ken was waiting. As the fear hit me again, I looked at my friends and said, "I don't know what it is, but something terrible is going to happen tonight." They looked at me as if I'd lost it, and *I* wondered if I had, too.

A few minutes later, a handsome man invited me to dance. I asked Pat to watch my purse while we danced. Returning to the table, I looked for my purse. I asked Pat if she'd moved it somewhere else, and then I realized why the voice had been warning me all day long: my purse—with my keys, driver's license, and credit cards—was gone!

Since my keys had been stolen, my friend John drove me home. I was horrified to find my front door unlocked, and it was even worse when we went inside: my possessions were strewn all over the floor. Whoever had stolen my purse had used my keys to enter my home, since my address was printed on my driver's license.

Although I look back on this incident and wonder why I didn't listen to the warning I'd been given, I'm grateful that it allowed me to meet my angels. And *now* I listen!

Once you get in the habit of listening, you'll be amazed and feel blessed by how the angels prove time and again that not only are they constantly around you, but they're forever on your side. Allow yourself to be empowered with the knowledge and wisdom of the messages they have for you. Judy Balcomb-Richey's story shows that this could even be a lifesaving decision:

One afternoon I drove home on my lunch hour. My apartment complex was deserted, as most people were at work. The complex consisted of four buildings with four apartments in each: two upstairs and two downstairs. I lived in one of the upstairs units.

I made my lunch and settled on the couch to watch TV and eat. I heard the door to our building creak open and footsteps coming upstairs. I thought that my downstairs neighbor Susan must have come home on her noon hour, too, and seen my car. We were old friends, and she'd sometimes come up to see me if we were both home for lunch at the same time. Sure enough, there was a knock on my door, and I jumped up to open it for her.

I suddenly heard a very clear voice in my right ear say, "Do not open that door!" I'd never experienced anything like this. The voice was so convincing that I approached the door and asked, "Who is it?"

A man's voice answered, "Telephone company."

I was on full alert by this time. "Yes, is there a problem?" I asked.

He stammered a little as he replied, "No, I just wanted to let you know that we will be doing work in the area and you may not have telephone service."

I thanked him, and I heard him start back down the stairs. He didn't knock on the other doors; he came straight to mine and no one else's. I later realized that he could have seen which apartment I went into from the window in the hallway at the top of the stairs. I looked to see if a service truck was parked outside, but there wasn't one.

When I returned to work, I called the phone company to ask if it would be common for a service technician to go door-to-door informing customers of a disruption of service. I later remembered that one week before this happened to me, a young female doctor had disappeared from her apartment. Her door was found open, but no signs of her were ever discovered. I didn't think too much of it at the time, but she did live less than two miles from me. It may not have been related at all, but at the very least I'm certain that the angel's voice saved me from being attacked . . . and possibly saved my life.

The angels are here not only to protect us, but also to reassure us. Making life-changing decisions can leave us feeling alone and vulnerable. Sometimes this can lead us to feel regret for having made the choices we did—it's so easy to forget why we decided to do the extreme things we do.

If you're struggling to come to a decision, remember to remain open to hearing the messages the angels have for you. Stay strong—know that you're loved and never alone and that when you're confident enough to listen, you'll always be guided to your true path, as Diana Sanders found:

I made a very difficult decision to leave my husband. My daughters, both college-age, were unhappy about this, even though they knew things between my husband and me were very bad. My youngest wouldn't even see me or talk to me.

I asked the angels for help, but things continued to get worse with my children. I was devastated. I didn't want to lose my relationship with them, and I began to question my decision and thought about returning home. But my inner voice kept saying, *Just be patient. Everything will be okay.*

Then one day as I was driving to work and crying about the difficulty with my daughters, I heard a clear voice say, "All is well. I am Gabriel."

I was startled. This was not an "inner voice," but a loud, audible, in-my-ear shouting! I wondered what was happening and thought that surely I must be losing it. *Gabriel?* I couldn't have heard *him*. But the voice said again, "I am Gabriel." I questioned my sanity. Then not only did I hear "I am Gabriel" a third time, but a truck zoomed past me and painted on its side were the words *Gabriel's Landscaping*.

From then on, I knew that everything would work out with my kids, and I never again doubted my decision. Sure enough, within days of that incident, my daughters and I were reconciled. It's not that we never again had difficult days, but I knew that if I put my relationship with them in Gabriel's care, all would be well.

It wasn't until I attended an angel seminar a couple of years later that I had an "Aha!" moment when I learned that Gabriel watches over children. I am so grateful for his continued help and guidance.

The angels hold our hands through physically and emotionally treacherous situations, protecting us from harm. Sometimes they need *our* help in doing so, though. That's when they give us can't-miss messages, such as the one that Christine Marsh received:

As I was getting ready to go home from high school, I received a very clear message from a male voice speaking just outside of my ear. He said, "Please be careful today when you are crossing the street."

Sure enough, as I was about to step out at an intersection on my way to the bus station to go home after school, I felt as though I were being gently held to the curb. A red van came speeding up, and by the time the driver was able to brake, he was in the middle of the crosswalk and had to back up to allow me to cross. If I had walked a few seconds earlier, I very likely would have been hit.

❖ ❖ ❖

In the next powerful story, Maureen O'Shea shares how beneficial it is to listen, and also to believe, the comforting messages that our guardian angels have for us:

I grew up Catholic during the era of hellfire and brimstone and good old Catholic guilt. However, I was blessed with an internal sense that God was more loving and less judgmental than the church at that time made it seem.

Still, I didn't realize how much God loved me until I was four months pregnant with my first child. My mother, who wrote for the local newspaper, felt compelled one day to tell me all of the stories she'd seen in the newsroom about babies being born with terrible deformities because their mothers had done drugs prior to pregnancy. Well, this was the 1970s, so of course I had tried some street drugs, like most young people back then.

After I heard those stories, I was a nervous wreck. I couldn't sleep, I could barely eat, and I was tense and anxious. Out of guilt and shame, I didn't feel that I could talk to anyone about my concerns. I certainly couldn't ask my doctor. This went on for maybe two months. Then one night as I was lying in bed staring at the ceiling, I heard a voice in my head—not a thought, but an actual voice—which clearly said: "It's a boy, and he's all right."

I knew that this message was from God. I slept the rest of that night with a peace I hadn't felt in months. The remaining weeks went by without another anxious thought. And when at the end of the nine months—and 20 hours of labor—the doctor announced, "It's a boy!" I said, "Of course it is!" And naturally my son was born perfectly healthy, as God had promised.

In addition to the voice of our guardian angels, we may also hear that of a loved one bringing us comfort and reassurance, as a woman named Brunella discovered:

My 51-year-old husband passed suddenly from a massive heart attack while playing basketball. Jim and I had been together since we were 18, and we had been married for 27 years.

Feeling so deeply numb at the news of his death, I sat on my couch just staring. My house was filled with family and friends who were trying to be supportive, but all I could do was stare in disbelief and shock. Suddenly, in my right ear I heard a quick, whispered utterance: "I love you."

It was fleeting and soft, but I heard the words as clearly as any other sound in the room. I didn't flinch or mention this to anyone because I knew that the message was meant for me alone. Those three little words helped ease some of my grief. And I thank my wonderful angels for helping me make this connection with my Jim.

Sometimes voices and messages can be accompanied by physical sensations such as a chill, as the following story from Anne Jay illustrates. The body knows and senses what's going to happen. Trust it!

A friend of mine lost his dog and searched everywhere, to no avail. When I heard about this, I started saying the prayer for a lost pet in Doreen's book *Healing with the Angels*. A year later, I was driving down the road where the dog was last seen. All of a sudden a chill went through me (this always happens when Archangel Michael is near), and I heard a voice say, "The dog has been found." This sensation stayed with me until I arrived home.

Later that day, I learned that my friend's dog had been found at noon, which was the exact time I had experienced the chill and heard the voice. Now I know that the angels always hear our prayers and miracles do happen!

In many of the stories in this book, including Anne Jay's, prayers are answered when people notice and follow their signs from above. Even in the most precarious situations we allow ourselves to get into, the angels are always there to offer us loving, nonjudgmental nudges toward safety and well-being. All we have to do is listen, as Jennifer Santiago discovered:

I was driving home late at night, feeling very tired. About half a mile from my house is a stoplight in an industrial area that's busy during the day but at night is completely deserted. While waiting for the light to turn green, I dozed off.

I suddenly heard what sounded like my mom's voice calling my name, which instantly woke me up. It was so loud and clear—as if she were in the car with me—but I was all alone, and my mother was at home. There weren't any other cars around, and my radio was off.

If it wasn't for the voice, I would have kept sleeping, and who knows what could have happened, since my car wasn't in the "park" gear. I believe that the voice was my guardian angel watching over me. Every day I give the angels thanks for taking care of me.

Hearing your name called by a disembodied voice is actually a common experience. This happens to most people as they're awakening from sleep, since that's when we're most open to hearing the angels.

Ever go somewhere and then get the urge to return home? Listen to that feeling when it arises. Too often we dismiss it because we confuse it with the guilt we feel for not being home when we truly deserve some time off. If the impulse comes to you and doesn't go away, make sure you take appropriate action. Fortunately, Carol Singleton listened to her angels when they urged her to go home:

My seven-year-old son, Scott, woke up at 5 A.M. with a stomachache. *Well, he did eat a lot of popcorn the night before,* I thought. I rested with him until my husband came home from work at the fire station at 9 A.M., yet Scott's stomach still hurt. After the three of us lay on the couch for a while, my husband suggested that I take myself out to lunch. With a firefighter husband who worked 24-hour shifts, I was a single mom for ten nights of the month. I didn't get a lot of alone time, so I appreciated the offer.

I was relaxing with a magazine after lunch at a local deli when loud and clear I heard a male voice say to me: "Go home!" I stopped reading, and again I heard, "Go home!" It was unlike anything I'd experienced before. So I knew that I should pay attention, and I went home.

When I arrived, there were two messages from my husband on the answering machine. The first one said that he and my son were at the doctor's office. The second informed me that they were at the hospital in the emergency room. When I got over there, my little guy was in a lot of pain and they were still doing tests.

I asked Scott, "Did you send me an angel to tell me to go home?"

He replied, "I don't know if I did, but I really *wanted* you to come home."

It was late in the afternoon on a Saturday, and it took a while for the on-call pediatric surgeon to arrive. Prior to surgery, they weren't positive what was causing the pain, and it turned out to be appendicitis. The surgeon said that Scott was the youngest child he had seen with this diagnosis. I have no doubt that an angel visited me, and I have always been grateful that he did.

Too often we dismiss true guidance with our own judgments and interpretations of situations. We're afraid of being wrong and so only make the "safest" decisions. Part of growing spiritually is realizing that our signs from above don't always make sense, as Cindy Felger experienced:

The house that I was living in had sold, and I had two weeks to move. Since I had three Australian shepherds and a cat, finding a rental with a yard for my dogs was a challenge. Of course that meant I needed to rent a house and not an apartment. At that time, I could only afford $700 a month.

Every day I'd call the newspaper ads about suitable homes, but every landlord said no to the dogs. Still, I kept praying and affirming that the Universe would provide me with the perfect place. Then I saw an ad for a house that seemed to have everything I wanted . . . and it was only $600 a month! My first thought was *This place must be a dump,* and I proceeded to dismiss it.

But then I heard a loving and firm male voice say, "Call!" I looked around and no one else was nearby. So I said "Okay" and dialed the number in the ad. A lovely woman answered the phone. I introduced myself, she gave me the address, and I drove immediately to the home. It was perfect!

I got the house, and my pets and I all lived very happily there for eight years.

Cindy was really glad that she bypassed her logic and trusted that the Universe always hears and answers every prayer. Her open-mindedness led her to a perfect house. If she hadn't heeded the Divine voice, she might have concluded that her angels weren't helping her or that she wasn't hearing their guidance.

Occasionally the extremes of life can make us feel out of control. Emotions can sometimes be hard to contain, but remember how powerful your angels are. Recall that you are on Earth to be loved, both by those here and those passed, as well as to love them in return. There is almost never a delay when you ask from your heart for help and comfort from the angels, as Joyce Meyers shares:

> My father had unexpectedly passed away two months earlier. It was just all too much for me to cope with, and now I was falling in love with the man who would eventually be my husband! I just couldn't deal with the myriad strong

emotions, and I worried that I was having a nervous breakdown.

One morning when things were especially intense, I sat at my desk and prayed for inner peace. As I did so, I began to physically feel a pulling from behind me, like I was being enfolded in a warm embrace. As I was held, I felt the anxiety dissolve in waves and leave my body, and I heard and felt the message: "Everything will be okay." In only a matter of seconds, my mind cleared and my body felt strong. Still, I was bewildered as to what had happened!

Afterward, I marveled at how much better I felt. My ability to cope had returned, and I once again had the strength to go on. I'd asked for celestial help, and the response was instantaneous. I know in my heart that we are all lovingly watched over.

● ● ●

The voice of God and the angels is that of love and wisdom. When they speak up, it's loud, clear, and unmistakable. In urgent situations the Divine voice is designed to get your attention in a hurry, so never worry that you'll miss this form of sign.

The angels want us to hear their messages, so they create many avenues by which to give us signs. In our next chapter, we'll look at one of the most common ways that angels convey them: through number sequences that we see in phone numbers and on license plates, clocks, receipts, and such.

III

Chapter Seven

ANGEL NUMBERS AS SIGNS

Numbers are often the most interesting—and sometimes, puzzling—signs to receive from the angels. Sequences appear in recurring patterns, and if you don't know what you're looking at, it can feel as if someone or something is out to confuse you.

Number signs come from all over. Most commonly, though, they're seen on clocks, license plates, and buildings; and in telephone numbers, e-mail time stamps, and cash-register totals. When you see repeating numbers in your life, ask your angels what they mean or look them up in the book *Angel Numbers 101,* which explains number meanings from 1 to 999 and covers any combination with more digits.

In this chapter, you'll read enchanting stories of how people have had their lives helped, changed, comforted, and reassured with the power of number signs. Our first story comes from Jason Simpson, who gets daily reminders that the angels are always with him:

> My angels send me signs in the form of number sequences that I see on license plates, receipts, clocks, and the like. For example, when I see the number 420, it's as if the angels are saying, "Hi, Jason," since my birthday is April 20. I keep a daily journal of angel numbers or other signs that I see. Sometimes I notice as many as 25 angel numbers in one day.

The joy of receiving particular numbers from the angels and the Universe can be so great that sharing the moment with someone can be just as powerful, or more so, for the other person. Angelica Montesano shares an example of how this is possible:

My friend Theresa taught me about the meaning of the number 11 and its patterns, like 111 or 1111. Although she didn't know the origin of her sentiments about this particular number, they had been there for as long as she could recall. She expressed high regard for the 11th day of each month—and even more so in November, when the date's numerical equivalent is 11/11. She had included the number 11 in the name of her production company and used it freely in all other projects and endeavors where numbers were called for.

One summer evening I was at a local mall shopping for household items. As I got ready to pay for an item at one of the stores, the cashier informed me that my total was $111.01. I took note of the number sequence, smirking silently. I moved on to the next store, and this time my total was exactly $111.

I immediately thought of Theresa and felt that it was important to call her on the spot. When I did, I was greeted by her voice mail and left a message explaining the sequence of numbers on my receipts that had led me to reach out to her.

When Theresa called back, she explained that at the time of my call, she'd been at the hospital mourning the death of her grandmother. She said that my 111 voice mail had been of great comfort to her. Whether it was an angel, the spirit of her grandmother, or the Divine Creator calling on me to be a friend that evening, I have no doubt that my message to Theresa was Divinely guided.

Angelica's story is a beautiful reminder to take action when we receive signs coupled with intuitive guidance. The number sequence 111 (and 1111) guides us to keep our thoughts positive and to only think about what we desire, rather than what we fear. However, there's no need to be afraid, for this number sequence is a reminder of the ever-present angels, as Cheryl Allen explains:

> Whenever I have doubts or questions, I receive a message from my angels. If I happen to glance at my clock and it reads 11:11, this reminds me that they love me and are always with me to help guide me on my path.

The angels, who always want you to be comfortable and happy, will also show you number signs to shield you from loss. When this happens, make sure to have love on your mind and in your heart when you think of passed loved ones or pets, because they are in your immediate presence, as this story from Renee Pisarz illustrates:

> When my beautiful son, Stephen, was killed in an automobile crash, I was

devastated. I'd always thought that death was final . . . until I began receiving clear signs from him in the form of numbers.

When my son played basketball in school, his jersey number was 54. He later used this number in his e-mail address. After Stephen's death, I started to see 54 everywhere as a sign of his ongoing love and presence.

For example, I'd notice 54 on clocks, license plates, and my car odometer. Even when I pulled into a metered parking spot, the minutes left would be his number. These were synchronicities, not coincidences. I picked up on the pattern. It always seemed like he was with me and I was being guided.

On my birthday I received a special gift. I stopped in front of a photo-frame shop, and in the window was a sports picture frame. I couldn't believe my eyes. It had a red sports jersey, and of course

the number on it was 54. A gift on my
birthday!

After the physical passing of my son,
my soul died and was reborn with my
new spiritual awareness.

Numbers can also give us the courage we need
to move forward and grow in our lives. A woman
named Avisha shares how number sequences
motivated her to follow her Divine guidance:

Recently I've been seeing the number
sequence 744 in various combinations,
which is an angel number that basically
means "You're on the right path! Keep up
the great work!" I know it's the angels'
way of giving me signs that I should keep
moving forward.

This was especially true one day when
I was driving to an intuitive Reiki session.
It would involve channeled messages
from angels, guides, and deceased loved
ones. I'd never had a psychic reading

before, and for some reason I was afraid
of receiving a message from my mother,
who'd passed away when I was a little
girl.

During the drive, I almost turned
around and went home because I was
afraid of hearing what I needed to hear.
Then a car drove past me with the number
474 on its license plate. I knew that this
was a sign from my angels reassuring me
that I was on the right path in going to
the Reiki session.

So in my mind I put a request out
to the angels. I said, *Please show me
another sign that lets me know that I should
go through with this reading.* Almost
immediately, another car passed me with
477 in its license plate. All fears left me
once I saw that number combination.

All in all, the reading was awesome,
and my mother had a lot of messages for
me. I felt that it healed me on a spiritual
level.

The angels are always around us, and no task is too small or petty for them. They're here to make our lives more peaceful and to help us stay on our true path so that we may learn the lessons we came here for. These lessons are evolutionary for our souls, so learning and growing are essential points of life.

In the next story, a woman named Robin shares how the angels made absolute certain that there was no doubt in her mind about their presence:

> As a doctoral student of educational psychology, I'd been looking for a different path and was very stressed at school and eager to start a career and end the academic chapter of my life.
>
> I yelled into the sky one night for someone to get me out of what I was doing or at least help me enjoy school. I longed to be helping people instead of spending endless hours in the classroom.

I began seeing triple numbers all around me. I saw them on license plates, the alarm clock, my cell phone, and the treadmill. I didn't know what they meant, but I thought it was odd that I'd woken up in the middle of the night more times than I could remember at 2:22, 3:33, and 4:44. I mentioned to my girlfriend that something very weird was going on and I needed to know what these numbers meant.

Eventually, I was drawn to Doreen's *Angel Numbers 101* book, which told me that 111 meant to keep a positive thought about your current situation. This led me to study angels and archangels.

Finally, it came time for me to teach, and I definitely asked the angels to help me. One day when I was passing out tests to my students, I mentioned that everyone had a guardian angel. I was a little nervous as I said this, because such topics are often not acceptable to discuss in a college setting outside of a theology course.

As she rubbed her arms, a girl in the front of the class remarked, "I think that is so cool. It gives me goose bumps." Another student said, "Me, too!"

As I handed out the final, without a second thought I told the students, "If you need a hand on the test, just call on Archangel Zadkiel because he is the 'Memory Archangel' who helps you remember things." My students smiled.

I walked back to my desk and opened my cell phone to switch it to silent mode. The time read 11:11. I thought, *Very clever, angels, very clever. My heart is forever open to, and grateful for, your messages of reassurance that I am not losing it!* In my mind's eye, I immediately saw Archangel Michael smile.

I don't know if it was Zadkiel's assistance in the room that day or just the study habits of my students, but all those who took the final that day got A's on the test.

Half the fun of finding numbers is searching for their meanings. When this first started happening to me (Charles), I felt as if I were a player in a huge game that I didn't remember asking to join. Sometimes it can feel odd, because the patterns and consistencies in the numbers are so absolute yet are encountered so randomly that they couldn't possibly be a coincidence. A woman named Pai Chideya shares a story about finding peace with number signs:

Right after I met a man whom I consider to be a soul mate, I started seeing the number 111 everywhere! I also started waking up at 2:22, 4:44, and 5:55. The numbers began driving me nuts because I knew that they meant something, but I didn't understand what.

Every time I'd turn my head or open a book, I'd see these numbers. I wondered what they signified but had no way of knowing.

Soon after, I began working for two new bosses. One was named Doreen, and the last name of the other was Virtue. That's why I was amazed when I found the book *Angel Numbers 101* by Doreen Virtue (whom I'd never heard of previously).

I began reading the book, and the numbers made perfect sense to me. They were like a form of communication with the angels that I didn't, and couldn't, control. Now I'm so in love with what's happening; and I truly feel guided by the angels, God, and the Universe. The more I trust, the more guidance I receive.

As with any other sign, you're always free to ask the angels to show you a number when you feel that it will help comfort or reassure you. The key to requesting a sign is not to push or force the timing of the angels. Don't stop to stare in places you normally wouldn't, or get frustrated if the number sign doesn't show up on a big billboard seconds after you ask. The timing is always Divine, and the angels will never let you down. Sometimes they just operate in their way, as Joyce O'Keeffe discovered:

I was going through a really difficult time mentally, physically, emotionally, and spiritually. Although I grew up in a positive household and spent many happy years at home, somewhere I'd lost faith in myself. When I looked in the mirror, I didn't recognize the reflection.

To feel better, a friend and I decided to go to a nightclub. I went through the motions of getting dressed, but I wasn't happy. Instead, my self-worth was nonexistent, and I felt like a prisoner of my own negative thoughts.

Fortunately, I still had the wherewithal to ask God for a sign. I said, "God, if I see the number 7 tonight, I'll know that this is a sign from You that everything will be okay." I don't know why I chose 7, but I did—and then promptly forgot about the prayer.

I put on a positive face and ventured out with my friend to the nightclub, where we danced. As we were leaving at the end of the night, a man I didn't know came up to me and said, "We are all 7s. I am 7. You are 7. Everything is 7!" I let him talk for about five minutes, awestruck by what I was hearing.

To me, he was an angel sent from God. I gave him a hug and said, "You don't know what this means to me!"

That's the night I realized that someone out there wanted me to carry on and remain hopeful. I shall always remember the magic from God and my forever-protecting angels.

Occasionally, numbers are signs about our deceased loved ones. These are usually not as general as the angel-number signs. Rather, they usually refer to something personally significant, such as a birth or anniversary date. Sometimes the angels send license plates that have the letters of the loved one's initials *plus* a significant number.

If you see numbers that remind you of someone, trust the meaning. As Lorraine Halica recounts in the following story, the numbers can be extremely healing:

My beloved husband, Peter, was taken to Heaven very unexpectedly. To deal with the grief, I decided to move to another state to be closer to my sister. My old house sold within a month, so I knew that I was making the right move.

My car's new license plates read: 505 WKS. It reminded me of 505 weeks, an easy-to-remember license plate.

But then my sister pointed out something to me that I hadn't considered: If Peter were still alive, he and I would have been married for 505 weeks!

Coincidence? I think not! I got a shiver, thanked God for this sign, and vowed never to turn in that license plate.

So far we've discussed signs from above, and you've read stories about the healings and discoveries of other people. But what about *you?* In the next two chapters, we'll look at ways in which you can get specific signs relating to your various life questions and concerns.

Chapter Eight

ASKING FOR A SIGN

Sure, signs are great way-showers, and they're often miraculous. But if they aren't coming to you automatically, how can you "activate" them in your life? Well, regardless of what rituals you may have heard of, communicating with the angels and asking them for signs is easier than reading this paragraph! Anytime you think, wish, will, or otherwise manifest something, you are praying for it and the angels are listening.

That's why it's important to monitor your thoughts and keep only what you *do* want on your mind at all times. Although the angels are around to help and to make sure you're on your correct path, they also understand that everyone is here to learn and evolve. Therefore, they'll be sure to accommodate you even when your thoughts aren't always in your own best interests.

This is because the law of energy is so absolute and complete in this Universe that it's our job to make sure only the highest, most positive and loving energy is allowed to flow through us. This isn't an overnight accomplishment, since our natural inclination is to handle everything ourselves and therefore dwell on whatever seems significant. So when we focus on bad things in our lives, we perpetuate negativity. This might sound like a catch-22, because how on earth are we supposed to solve anything if we can't process it? That's where the angels come in. . . .

Have you ever heard the saying "Let go and let God"? If there were ever truer words to live by, *we* haven't heard them. One of the most amazing and blessed things about having angels around us is that they'll do almost anything to ensure that our lives are happy, fulfilled, and in the light. They also make certain we're comforted in times of need, given a sense of companionship when we feel alone, and lent strength when we feel weak or helpless. And for all of this help, the angels ask nothing more in return than for us to be happy and believe that they exist.

Here are steps you can follow whenever you'd like the angels to send you a sign of comfort or guidance.

The Steps to Receiving Signs from Above

1. Ask. Because of the Law of Free Will, the angels can only help you—including giving you signs—if you ask. So, if you want a sign, you must ask for one. It's best not to specify what type you want to appear. Instead, just notice the repetitive patterns that occur after you put in your request.

Although rituals aren't necessary, they can be helpful because we're all creatures of habit. If we can make a routine and an instinct out of communicating with our angels, then our lives become blessed beyond imagination. Thinking is a form of prayer, and realizing this will help us make sure that all of the requests we place with our angels are the ones we actually want.

A woman named Louise shares how asking for a sign helped her find peace in a traumatic situation. Now she receives regular, yearly signs that everything is okay.

> We were devastated when our three-week-old son, Ricky, was diagnosed with a rare heart condition. Soon afterward, he passed away in my husband's arms.
>
> A few days after Ricky died, my husband had to go back to work. I didn't know many other people where we lived, so I didn't really have anyone else to talk to. It was a desperately lonely and sad time. One afternoon about a week after Ricky had left us, I was sitting in front of our house with my husband. I was so sad, and I said to him, "If only I had a sign that he is okay. I just want to know that he's being cared for and that he's happy and not in pain anymore."

Just then our eldest daughter came running and shouting for us to go to the backyard. When we ran out back, there was the most spectacular rainbow straight over our yard. It was huge, and the colors were so bright! Although the rainbow was exceptionally beautiful, I thought that it was just a coincidence.

Then, as if to convince me that it *wasn't,* it started to snow—just softly, with tiny flakes that landed really gently. We stood with our arms out, simply looking up at the snow falling, watching it melt on our skin, and gazing at each other in disbelief. It was on a bright sunny afternoon, and snow was just out of the question.

I asked other people if they saw the snow on that day, and they just looked at me like I was mad. I rang my sister and told her—she thought that the grief was too much for me and suggested that I see a counselor. But I knew that it really did happen, and it was a sign. Although we were the only ones who saw the snow, it gave me much peace, and I was able to move forward.

We also receive signs that Ricky is fine from the miniature yellow rosebush that I planted right before he died. Every year on the anniversary of his death and his birthday, I always get a new bud. To me, these yellow rosebuds are my angels' way of letting me know that my son is okay.

2. Have faith. Trust that the angels are with you, and have faith in the signs that they send. Michelle Simmonds shows us that just asking and believing is often sign enough, and that faith is a very powerful tool:

> I was living in my new adopted city of Melbourne, Australia, and I didn't know many people. So when a workmate kindly invited me to a party, I gladly accepted.

As I was driving there, it was very cold and dark.

Although I'd been given directions, I was soon lost in the winding streets of a deserted industrial area. I was frightened, especially since I didn't have a cell phone or a map with me, so I prayed to God and my angels to please help me. I immediately felt a sense of calm come over me.

I kept driving and followed my intuition, as I could feel God and the angels guiding me. Soon I was on a main road, where there was a fast-food restaurant. I went to the drive-through, made a small purchase, and asked for directions. As I came out of the driveway, I saw a church across the road, and when I read their notice board, I burst out laughing. It said: "Lost? Let God show you the way!"

3. Trust in Divine timing. Every prayer is heard and answered, but sometimes the fulfillment seems delayed as the angels work behind the scenes to orchestrate the details.

Heather Succio's story illustrates how requests and prayers are answered exactly when they're supposed to be:

I only knew Grandpa Davis for the first six years of my life, which are those formative years when any kindness has a profound impact. My grandpa was my buddy. He constantly made a point of being there for me and doing little things that make such a huge difference in the life of a five-year-old child. For instance, he fashioned me a witch's nose out of Silly Putty one Halloween and made sure to be there to take me out for my first trick-or-treat extravaganza! He made me a school-year scrapbook, with report cards, pictures, kindergarten worksheets, and drawings lovingly pasted in with handwritten captions.

My grandpa was also an avid stamp collector. He was fascinated by them—foreign or domestic, pristine or battered. He gathered, pasted, and proudly displayed countless postage stamps in books and boxes, which seemed to be bursting out of every storage closet in my parents' house. He simply loved the look of them and their connection to exotic travel destinations.

Although he worked for the airlines, he was "grounded" in the mechanic's shed. I've often thought that he must have had a romantic wanderer's heart, fantasizing about where he might go someday. After he passed away, I trusted that he was there somewhere "up above," although I wasn't able to touch, hear, or see him.

Feeling particularly wistful one evening, I pleaded for my grandpa to say hello. I knew not to ask for something specific. I just prayed that I'd know he was there, but by something more tangible than simply a feeling in my heart.

The morning after I asked my grandpa for that sign—12 hours after pleading for some indication of his presence in my life—a postal package arrived. As I was sitting at the breakfast table, my husband said, "A package that I'd ordered arrived this morning—from Hong Kong, of all places! The entire box is absolutely covered top to bottom, left to right, with these incredibly beautiful postage stamps. Do you know anybody who collects them?"

My eyes filled with tears as I first thanked my husband, then my grandpa. Isn't life so precious and so wonderful, especially when we can know that we aren't going through it alone? Ask, and ye shall receive . . . even signs from above! Although I've always felt loved and protected by the angels, it's wonderful to get confirmation.

As Heather's story reveals, some prayers are answered immediately, while others can take a while. But the angels always hear and respond to every request for help.

4. Notice the signs. If you've asked for signs and believe you haven't yet received one, it could be that you haven't noticed or trusted those that have been delivered. Not to worry, though, as there's an endless supply! Ask the angels for other signs, and request that they help you recognize and understand them.

The angels are happy to keep repeating signs until you notice them. Even if you don't grasp the meaning of one, noticing it is important. It's a good idea to ask the angels to explain what it means, in addition to trusting your gut feelings and ideas about its significance.

Bev Black's fears were allayed because she trusted the lights that she saw (which, by the way, are a common sign that the angels are with you, protecting and overseeing you and your situation):

I was driving to pick up my husband at the Bellingham Airport. I'd traveled on two Canadian ferries and was now on the last leg of my journey from British Columbia to Washington.

The highway was already snowy and icy when a huge storm hit with thunder, lightning, and then hailstones so big and thick that I could barely see in front of me. There was no place to pull over, as the road was narrow and dark.

I got really scared and started asking my angels to protect me and get me to my destination. Within minutes, I saw bright flashes of light right beside me on the car passenger seat and knew that my prayers had been answered. I had an angel sitting there keeping me calm and offering support. I drove the rest of the way calmly and with confidence, knowing that I didn't have to be afraid any longer.

5. Take action when guided. Signs from above often give you messages about actions you can take to bring about the answer to your prayers. As Lisa Hopp discovered, it's important to act upon this guidance:

I was having a very difficult day and didn't know how to cope. As I was driving to my parents' house, I looked up at the sky and screamed out loud: "How do I get out of this mess?!"

A gray Volkswagen van approaching on my left caught my eye. The way that it passed me attracted my attention more than the van itself at first: it came up fairly quickly, then seemed to lose speed once it passed.

The van had a white bumper sticker with purple flowers, and there was writing on the lower part of it. Since purple is my favorite color, this stood out to me. The bumper sticker read: "Simply Simplify." Unbelievably, as soon as I read it, the van sped up and drove off over a small hill in front of me. Seconds later, I drove over the same hill, but the van was gone from sight.

My gut told me that I'd just received an answer to my earlier prayer through this sign, but mentally I didn't understand the message and emotionally I didn't believe that I was worthy of this intervention, so I blew it off as a coincidence.

Two hours later, I was back at home in the living room, reading the Sunday paper. The television in front of me was tuned in to the first football game of the day. I laid each section of the newspaper out in front of me for better access to the ones that interested me.

The real-estate section was to the left. My attention kept going in that direction, and I didn't understand why. I even found myself picking it up, looking at the front, and putting it back down. Twice I did this before I finally succumbed to the urge and opened the first page. On the inside bottom left was a drawing of large, luxurious homes. Written on the front of these beautiful homes in big script were the words *Simply Simplify.*

Before I had time to react to these words, the volume on my television went up considerably on its own. I looked up instantly to watch the two football commentators on the screen. The first one said, "How do you think he was able to make these changes to the offense?"

The other commentator replied, "I know exactly how he made these changes: he *simply simplified* the offensive line."

Then the volume went back down. I began to cry. I thanked my angels and asked them to help me understand this message and make the necessary changes. Since then, I've simplified my life in various ways, and it has helped me cope—as well as hear my angels even better.

Other Ways to Get Signs

— **Say your prayer aloud.** If quietly thinking your thoughts or desires doesn't yield a fulfilled or secure feeling, try saying your prayer out loud. Although it makes no difference to the angels, how *you* feel about your form of expression is almost as important as the actual act of doing it. This is because if you don't feel confident that you've given your problems away to the angelic realm, you may still be tempted to focus on them (and you know what negative attention can bring). Saying a prayer aloud with confidence is a wonderful way to let go of worry.

— **Write down your prayer.** Another powerful form of communicating is to write down your thoughts on paper or type them on your computer. This is so effective because not only does it allow you to express yourself completely, but if you save your prayer, it also serves as a physical reminder that you've already dealt with this issue by giving it to the angels. Your writing doesn't have to be legible, chronological, grammatically correct, or even in complete sentences. Your feelings when you write are what's most important.

— **Meditate upon your prayer.** Meditation allows you to completely express your thoughts. I (Charles) frequently meditate when I have a question or request on my mind. As I fall deeper into the meditation, I ask the angels to take all thoughts from me and lovingly manage them for me. My rule for this meditation is that I can't return to reality until my mind is empty of all thoughts and emotions. When I come back from the meditation, I'm left with a feeling of complete relaxation. I've also rid myself of those pesky thoughts that wait until nothing else is on your mind to start pestering you; you know the ones I mean: *Did I pay that bill? . . . I wonder what she meant by that earlier. . . . My feet hurt*—the thoughts that prevent you from knowing *true* peace.

— **Visualize your prayer being answered.**

One more extremely effective way not only to communicate your wishes to the angelic realm, but also to help you become ever more powerful with your manifestation is to visualize what you want as already accomplished and complete. When you set out on a goal, know that you can do it, see the end product of your effort, and don't allow yourself to focus on any fear or doubt about the details.

● ● ●

The next time you have an issue, use whatever technique works best for you and your immediate circumstances in order to ask the angels to take this problem away from you and solve it. Be patient, as the timing of Heaven is not bound by our clocks; instead, it's guided by divinity. Remember that if you begin to doubt the ability of the angels even after you know they've taken a task from you, you can halt the entire process because they think that you may not want their help anymore.

Whatever method you choose, whatever you wish for, remember that the angels are not here to always take action *for* us, but rather to lead *us* to the necessary actions for the betterment and growth of our souls. This is why signs are so important—they're all around us, and if we open ourselves up to them in whatever form they may take, our lives are that much more peaceful and harmonious.

Use all of your senses in order to notice the signs, which are *always* delivered in response to your request. So you may receive your sign visually, through your feelings, as a voice or music that you hear, as an idea that pops into your mind, or even through your sense of smell, as Krista's story illustrates:

> Although I'm only 11 years old, I've always had a strong connection with the spirits around me. When I stayed at my grandmother's house, I could always see them and feel them playfully.
>
> Sometimes I feel empty for not being

able to help the world. I feel useless and depressed. But when that happens, I get a momentary strong smell of smoke. Instead of scaring me, it makes me feel comforted.

I finally talked with my mother about this. That's when I found out that my great-grandfather smoked, and the smell was a sign that he was with me and comforting me. I thank him greatly for his help.

Signature scents, such as Krista's great-grandfather's cigarette smoke, are signs of a departed loved one's presence and happiness. And sometimes, as a woman named De Williams discovered, a personally meaningful fragrance can also be a sign of Divine guidance:

I asked the angels for physical confirmation of their presence as well as of the fact that I did indeed have psychic abilities that I could develop. Days went by with no word or hint of anything. I'd started using the *Messages from Your Angels Oracle Cards* and kept getting the card that indicated a deceased loved one was trying to contact me. Not having a clue who this could be, I'd asked for clarification on that as well.

I work with my father-in-law, who owns his own company, so our office is in his house. I came to work on a Wednesday morning, and when I walked into the living room, I caught the scent of a man's cologne and instantly thought of my own father, as it smelled just like the kind he wears. I hadn't known my father-in-law to wear cologne, but I didn't know that he *never* did, so I dismissed the scent. I kept smelling it strongly periodically throughout the morning in different parts of the house. The cologne was noticeable no matter what room I was in. I even wondered if this was a "hint" related to the deceased-loved-one card. But the fragrance was so strongly associated with my dad, who was alive and well, that I decided that this couldn't be the case.

It was after that thought that I heard a voice in my head say, *Call your dad and make sure he's okay.* Now I get wrong premonitions and gut feelings all the time, so I decided that my dad was fine and I was being paranoid. Again, I dismissed the thought, like I had the scent.

Later I went to the bookstore. As I was standing in the aisle looking at the *Archangels & Ascended Masters* book, the scent of cologne hit me again. There wasn't anybody, let alone a man, around me. No one walked by. I smelled it on more than one occasion that afternoon while I was outside in the yard at home. This time I even smelled my shirt (even though I knew better) to see if maybe it was something on *me*. I found nothing.

I dismissed the incident again, and that was the last time I smelled the cologne.

The next day I sent my dad a joke e-mail and, surprisingly, received an e-mail back (he rarely communicated with me). He told me that he'd had to have his heart shocked the day before. I called him to find out what had happened. He'd been at the doctor's office and his heart had gone into atrial fibrillation. He was sent to the emergency room, where he didn't respond to medication, so they'd had to stop his heart and shock it back into rhythm.

I told my dad about smelling his cologne the day before and how I'd almost called him to find out if he was okay. He then informed that he *had* worn cologne the day before, and that it was the first time he'd put it on in many months. I asked him when the whole heart-fibrillation event happened, as I'd really smelled the scent frequently from the hours of 9 A.M. to noon. He told me that it all started at 9:30 A.M. He said that he felt fine now, was back at work, and had an appointment the next day with a cardiologist.

My father has problems with high blood pressure but had never had anything wrong with his heart! So I went home and had a talk with the angels. I apologized for ignoring their warning about my father. I asked for healing for him—specifically, that his cardiologist would give him a clean bill of health.

I called my dad after his appointment, and he *had* been told there was nothing wrong with his heart. They couldn't find a cause for the atrial fibrillation, and his heart was healthy. I don't doubt the angels' presence anymore. I *know* they're there.

Signs can also come through other people, so it's important to pay attention when someone's words ring true. What was spoken may have been delivered directly from the angels (and usually the other person doesn't even realize the Earth-angel role that he or she just played). It's a matter of trusting what you hear, as Rosalinda "Chayito" Champion realized when she heard the same message from two different people:

> I'm a professional flamenco singer who was raised within a family of artists. I guess I've always known that music, angels, and God were all interconnected. I've received Divine guidance many times to sing for and about God but have ignored the call for the last 20 years.
>
> Recently I was singing in a lounge where there was a jumble of noise, liquor, and high spirits. Three ladies dressed in white walked in and said that they wanted to watch my show and possibly hire me for their father's birthday party. When I finished, they invited me over to their table, held my hand, and started praying for me. I looked around, but no

one was watching us. I closed my eyes; and they kept praying for my strength, health, direction, and so on.

When they finished, one of them said, "I have a message for you from God. You've been molded and shaped with much suffering for all these years. Chayito, you are to sing for Him now— with your powerful voice, sing His message and His praise."

I was in awe of how God came to me in the middle of a San Antonio lounge! Three weeks later, though, I'd forgotten about the whole thing. Then the sisters returned with several more ladies dressed in white, and one of the eldest said, "I have a message for you from God: you need to start writing lyrics and music so that you can sing His message and praise."

The lady who'd spoken to me on the previous occasion turned and said, "I gave her that same message three weeks ago. I hadn't shared that with you, so this is a true confirmation."

I feel that the angels and God sent those wonderful ladies, and that after years of asking about my purpose, He revealed it to me. I am following through with this guidance, with the help of Archangel Gabriel. I now believe that there are Earth angels, and I met six of them a month ago.

In the next chapter, you'll read suggestions for prayers that will help you receive signs for specific life issues.

● ● ●   ● ● ●

Chapter Nine

PRAYERS FOR SIGNS

The words you use are secondary to the purpose behind your prayers. That's because angels respond to your intentions. So you can ask for career or relationship guidance, for example, in thousands of different ways. Yet what the angels pay attention to are your underlying emotions. Are you asking for peace, security, excitement, or bliss? That's what the angels will bring to you.

The angels answer most prayers by giving you signs and other forms of Divine guidance (such as intuitive feelings or repetitive ideas). When you notice and follow these signs, all the doors of opportunity and peacefulness subsequently open, as you've read about throughout this book.

In this chapter, we'll look at some examples of prayers that you can use to elicit signs for various life areas. You can say them aloud, silently, in song, in writing, or any other way you can dream of. Again, the form of your prayer isn't significant compared to these three steps:

1. Ask. Remember that the angels can only give you signs if you request them.

2. Notice the signs when they occur. Related to this is trusting that the signs aren't coincidental. If you doubt the validity of the ones you come across, repeat #1 above and ask for a sign that what you're receiving is real.

3. Follow through on the guidance imparted by the signs. If your angels' signs ask you to take action, then you must do so before your prayer can be fulfilled.

Let's begin with a general prayer for signs:

Dear Angels,

I ask that you give me clear signs in the physical world that I will easily notice and understand in order to help me with [describe the situation or question].

This prayer requests that your signs come to you concretely and that you're able to recognize them.

Now, here's a prayer to help you follow through on the Divine guidance inherent within the signs:

Dear Angels,

Please give me the courage and motivation to take action as you have guided me.

The following sections contain more prayers for signs in specific situations. Feel free to alter or add to them or create ones of your own. Remember that the angels hear and answer every prayer—from everyone (and that includes *you*).

Prayers for Blessings and Protection

Prayer for Children

Dear Angels,

Please show me a sign that love surrounds my children. Please send them my caring and blanket them in your protective energy. I ask that you please show me clear and obvious signs when it is time for me to help or intervene in any way for the benefit of their development.

Prayer for Your Spouse

Dear Angels,

Please watch over and protect my spouse, and show me a sign that everything is going to be okay in our relationship. I ask this not out of insecurity, but as a loving reminder that I am on the right path.

Prayer for Your Parents

Dear Angels,

Thank you for watching over my mother and father . . . guiding, protecting, and helping them. Please give me a clear sign of their love and happiness, and send me guidance if I am to take action to help them or be helped by them.

Prayer for a Pet

Dear Angels,

Please watch over my pet and ensure my beloved animal's safety, health, and happiness. Thank you for giving me clear signs that enable me to better understand my pet's needs.

Prayer for a Lost Pet

Dear Angels,

I know that no one and nothing can truly ever be lost, since you can see everything and everyone. I affirm that nothing is lost in the eyes of God. I ask that you help me reunite with my pet right now. I call upon you to send a signal so that I may find my pet. I now relax, knowing that you, God, and my higher self are already communing with my pet.

Prayer for a Friend

Dear Angels,

Please help my friend [name of person] *find peace within—and within this situation. Please give me easily distinguishable signs that indicate how to best support and help my friend.*

Prayers for Conflict Resolution

Prayer for Healing a Disagreement with a Loved One

Dear Angels,

Please give me a sign that there is a peaceful and harmonious solution to this conflict I have encountered. Please let love and forgiveness surround us, and guide us back into each other's arms.

Prayer for Communicating with Children

Dear Angels,

Please give me a sign that what I have to say makes a difference to my children. Please send my love and protection to them, and know that I only want the best for them.

Prayer for Resolving an Argument with a Neighbor

Dear Angels,

Please show me a sign that there is a solution to this situation with my neighbor. We share the same general location—and therefore the same general energy—and I want to make sure we are both sending only light and love into it.

Prayer for Easing Tension with In-Laws

Dear Angels,

Please show me a sign that everything will work out and that I will find peace with the parents of my spouse. I am in love with their child, and I want my partner's mother and father to know that I only have the best intentions for the relationship.

Prayer for Resolving Trouble in the Workplace

Dear Angels,

Please give me a sign that I will once again find happiness at work or that I am intended for a different position. Please guide me to my next step, either by helping me resolve my current issues or by showing me that it is time to move on.

Prayers for Health

Prayer for Healing Addictions

Dear Angels,

Please release me from cravings for [name of addiction] and help me feel fulfilled and peaceful naturally. Thank you for giving me clear signs to guide my behavior in healthful directions.

Prayer for Healing an Illness

Dear Angels,

My greatest prayer is for peace on every level: physically, emotionally, mentally, intellectually, and spiritually. Please give me signs as to how I can best improve my health in all of these areas.

Prayer for Adopting a Healthful Lifestyle

Dear Angels,

Thank you for giving me clear signs as to how to live a healthful lifestyle. Please guide my eating, drinking, exercise, sleep, and all other aspects of healthy living.

Prayer for Healing a Grieving Heart

Dear Angels,

Thank you for helping my heart heal from grief. Please send me a sign to let me know that my loved one is doing well in Heaven and [add anything else you'd like to know about the person].

Prayer for Losing Weight and Getting Fit

Dear Angels,

I am ready to release excess, unhealthy weight from my body and my life. Please give me signs and guidance as to the healthiest and most effective weight-loss methods for my personality, budget, and schedule.

Prayer for a Loved One's Health

Dear Angels,

I ask that you give extra attention, love, and care to [name of person] and nurse my loved one back to health. Please give me signs of reassurance, as well as guidance on how I can best support [name]'s health.

Prayer for Recovering from an Injury

Dear Angels,

Thank you for helping my body regenerate miraculously fast. Please give me signs that my recovery is going well, along with guidance about the steps that I can take.

Prayers Around the House

Prayer for Finding Lost Items

Dear Angels,

Please show me a sign to help me find my lost [name of item]. I feel that it is around here somewhere, and I just need a small sign to point me in the right direction.

Prayer for Moving into a Wonderful New Home

Dear Angels,

Thank you for giving me signs about whether I should move and the best place for me to go. Please guide me in all aspects of this proposed move, and help me notice and follow your signs.

Prayer for Protecting Possessions

Dear Angels,

Please show me a sign that while I am away my house and all of its possessions will remain safe from unwanted outside intrusion. If there is anything I can do to further protect my household, please give me an appropriate sign.

Prayers for Life Purpose, Career, and Finances

Prayer for Changing Careers

Dear Angels,

I am in need of your counsel about my career choice. Please send me signs and guidance as to the best profession to fulfill my emotional, spiritual, financial, and intellectual needs.

Prayer for Financial Security

Dear Angels,

Thank you for guiding me clearly to the steps that I can take to gain true financial security. I appreciate your giving me signs to help me feel secure about my money situation and to let me know that you are assisting me with my finances.

Prayer for Finding Your Life Purpose

Dear Angels,

I would like to know my purpose here on Earth and how I can incorporate that mission into a wonderfully fulfilling career that will support me financially. Please send me clear signs that I will easily notice and understand to guide me to my true life purpose.

Prayer for Paying the Bills

Dear Angels,

Please give me reassuring signs that my bills will be paid, and guide me as to how to increase my income and decrease my expenditures. Thank you for helping me pay all of my bills easily, effortlessly, and with money left over to spare and share.

Prayer for Self-Employment

Dear Angels,

Thank you for giving me signs to guide me along the path of self-employment. I appreciate your giving me ideas, connections, financial support, and [name anything else that you need] *to help me with entrepreneurship.*

Prayers for Love Life

Prayer for Attracting Your Soul Mate

Dear Angels,

Thank you for giving me signs that lead me to my soul mate. Please help me recognize and follow them to better prepare me for my wonderful love partnership.

Prayer for Healing Your Heart

Dear Angels,

I need your support, comfort, reassurance, and love. Please help me release sadness, grief, bitterness, and disappointment. Please give me clear signs that my heart is healing and that everything is okay.

Prayer for Attracting Love

Dear Angels,

I would appreciate your intervention into my love life so that I feel fulfilled romantically. Please guide me with signs so that I can take appropriate steps to increase the romance in my life.

Prayer for Knowing
Whether to Leave or Stay

Dear Angels,

I am confused as to whether to leave my current relationship or not. Please give me signs to help me make the decision with love and clarity.

Prayer for Recognizing Your Soul Mate

Dear Angels,

I need to know if [name of person] is my soul mate. Please give me clear signs to help me discern whether this person and relationship will culminate in the romantic partnership that I desire.

Prayers for Manifesting

Prayer for Attracting New Friends

Dear Angels,

Thank you for helping me attract wonderfully fun, supportive, healthy, interesting [name any other character-istics that are important to you] *new friends. Please give me signs pointing me in the right direction toward my new friendships.*

Prayer for Creating Abundance

Dear Angels,

I am ready to stand in the flow of financial abundance, and I ask that you send me clear signs as to my best course of action to attract this prosperity. Please help me recognize, understand, and follow these signs.

Prayer for Making a Decision

Dear Angels,

    I need help deciding between [name of first option] *and* [name of second option], *and I would like your signs and guidance as to which direction will lead to my greatest amount of peace.*

AFTERWORD

As we've explored throughout this book, signs come in many different forms and situations. They are deeply personal, and what's significant to you may not make sense in another person's life. Signs always need to be put into the context of the question you asked prior to receiving them.

Using the powerful guidance of signs can alleviate anxiety and control issues. After all, trying too hard to make something happen can end up working *against* your desires. The harder you push, the more difficult it can seem.

This principle seems to hold true in many different parts of life. One extreme example is how skydivers avoid injury upon impact with the ground by relaxing their bodies and rolling with the force. Those who tense up and try to control their falls usually end up with some sort of trauma as a result. Our bodies are made to work best when relaxed and at ease.

The world improves as we all improve individually. As complex as life on this planet may seem, it's just a mass collection of individuals on unique paths who are only trying to get by. In the past, people believed that suffering was an inherent part of life and work. Not anymore, though! The angels have been such a huge presence lately because they know that we can better the world and ourselves.

By letting go of our fears, worries, and controlling natures, we all live happier, safer, and more beneficial lives. Ask the angels to show you signs that they're here with you. After you receive validation, take this a step further by asking the angels to guide you as to your next move, or ask them to confirm that you're on the right path. You'll definitely receive your sign, and once you truly believe that the signs are there and learn to recognize them, your life will be more fulfilled and blessed than you can imagine.

We'll be with you in spirit every step of the way.

Love,
Doreen and Charles

ABOUT THE AUTHORS

Doreen Virtue holds B.A., M.A., and Ph.D. degrees in counseling psychology, and is a lifelong clairvoyant who works with the angelic realm. She is the author of the *Healing with the Angels* book and oracle cards; *Archangels & Ascended Masters;* and *Angel Therapy*®, among other works. Her products are available in most languages worldwide.

Doreen has appeared on *Oprah*, CNN, *The View,* and other television and radio programs. She writes regular columns for *Woman's World, New Age Retailer,* and *Spirit & Destiny* magazines. For more information on Doreen and the workshops she presents, please visit **www.AngelTherapy.com.**

You can listen to Doreen's live weekly radio show, and call her for a reading, by visiting **HayHouseRadio.com**®.

Charles Virtue is the eldest son of Doreen Virtue and is a teacher of Working with Your Angels. Charles has always placed high emphasis on the power of thoughts and how they are manifested into reality. After working with and around his mother and assisting with her certification courses for more than seven years, he now teaches his own classes throughout the world.

For more information about Charles and his teachings, audio books, and other products, please visit his Website at: **www.CharlesVirtue.com**. There you will find a complete bio, photographs, a calendar of events, and information on arranging an angel reading with him.

NOTES

NOTES

NOTES

NOTES

NOTES

NOTES

ALSO AVAILABLE

Books/Kits/Oracle Board

Angel Blessings Candle Kit
(*includes booklet, CD, journal, etc.*)
Angel Medicine
Angel Numbers 101
Angel Therapy
The Angel Therapy® Handbook
(*available May 2010*)
Angel Visions
Angel Visions II
Angels 101
Archangels & Ascended Masters
The Art of Raw Living Food
(*with Jenny Ross; available August 2009*)
Break the Pattern of Yo-Yo Dieting Forever!
The Care and Feeding of Indigo Children
Chakra Clearing
Connecting with Your Angels Kit
(*includes booklet, CD, journal, etc.*)

Audio/CD Programs

Connecting with Your Angels
Goddesses & Angels (*abridged audio book*)
Healing Your Appetite, Healing Your Life
Karma Releasing

Oracle Cards
(44 or 45 divination cards and guidebook)

Angel Therapy® Oracle Cards
(*available December 2009*)
Archangel Michael Oracle Cards
Archangel Oracle Cards
Ascended Masters Oracle Cards
Daily Guidance from Your Angels Oracle Cards
Goddess Guidance Oracle Cards
Healing with the Fairies Oracle Cards
Magical Mermaids and Dolphins Oracle Cards
Magical Messages from the Fairies Oracle Cards
Magical Unicorns Oracle Cards
Saints & Angels Oracle Cards

All of the above are available at your local
bookstore, or may be ordered by visiting:

Hay House UK: www.hayhouse.co.uk
Hay House USA: www.hayhouse.com®
Hay House Australia: www.hayhouse.com.au
Hay House South Africa: www.hayhouse.co.za
Hay House India: www.hayhouse.co.in

Doreen's Website: www.AngelTherapy.com

MESSAGES FROM SPIRIT: The Extraordinary Power of Oracles, Omens, and Signs,
by Colette Baron-Reid

PAST LIVES, PRESENT MIRACLES,
by Denise Linn

THE 7 SECRETS OF SOUND HEALING,
by Jonathan Goldman

We hope you enjoyed this Hay House book.
If you would like to receive a free catalogue featuring additional
Hay House books and products, or if you would like information
about the Hay Foundation, please contact:

Hay House UK Ltd
292B Kensal Rd • London W10 5BE
Tel: (44) 20 8962 1230; Fax: (44) 20 8962 1239
www.hayhouse.co.uk

***

Published and distributed in the United States of America by:
Hay House, Inc. • PO Box 5100 • Carlsbad, CA 92018-5100
Tel.: (1) 760 431 7695 or (1) 800 654 5126;
Fax: (1) 760 431 6948 or (1) 800 650 5115
www.hayhouse.com

Published and distributed in Australia by:
Hay House Australia Ltd • 18/36 Ralph St • Alexandria NSW 2015
Tel.: (61) 2 9669 4299; Fax: (61) 2 9669 4144
www.hayhouse.com.au

Published and distributed in the Republic of South Africa by:
Hay House SA (Pty) Ltd • PO Box 990 • Witkoppen 2068
Tel./Fax: (27) 11 467 8904 • www.hayhouse.co.za

Published and distributed in India by:
Hay House Publishers India • Muskaan Complex • Plot No.3
B-2 • Vasant Kunj • New Delhi – 110 070.
Tel.: (91) 11 41761620; Fax: (91) 11 41761630.
www.hayhouse.co.in

Distributed in Canada by:
Raincoast • 9050 Shaughnessy St • Vancouver, BC V6P 6E5
Tel.: (1) 604 323 7100; Fax: (1) 604 323 2600

***

Sign up via the Hay House UK website to receive the Hay House
online newsletter and stay informed about what's going on with
your favourite authors. You'll receive bimonthly announcements
about discounts and offers, special events, product highlights,
free excerpts, giveaways, and more!
www.hayhouse.co.uk